I Am Here

"I truly related with so many aspects of Ashley's life that she so beautifully shared in *I Am Here*. I'm so grateful to have read her powerful words and believe everyone can take something beneficial from them."

—Rachel Platten, Emmy Award winner, multiplatinum-selling
recording artist, and author

"In *I Am Here*, Ashley made the process of moving from the rocky, uncertain side of our pain over to the expansive side of flourishing not only accessible but possible. The process may not be easy (the good stuff rarely is), but Ashley laid out a road map which leads to hope and joy despite it all, even because of it all. She is a trustworthy guide who lives what she preaches. Let her grab you by the hand and walk you toward wholeness."

—Jen Hatmaker, *New York Times* bestselling author, speaker,
and podcast host

"If you are stuck and wanting to live a better life, Ashley is here to help you in this beautiful book, *I Am Here*. I know from personal experience and my friendship with Ashley how powerful her Clarity Mapping tool is and how real her story is. I know this book will give you the jump start or the restart you need to start living intentionally!"

—Mallory Ervin, author of *Living Fully*, founder of the Living Fully™
lifestyle brand, and host of the *Living Fully* podcast

"Ashley's words resonate so deeply in my heart, as I know they will in every woman's heart who finds herself enraptured by these pages. My story is different from hers, yet so similar and with the same basic challenges, fears, and questions we all have about ourselves. Her honesty, encouragement, and instruction are life-changing! I imagine my copy of this book being marked up and dog-eared like a favorite well-worn cookbook because I see myself going back to it over and over again!"

—Kimberly Schlapman, singer-songwriter of Little Big Town and author of *Oh Gussie!*

"A beautiful reflection on what it means to truly find yourself and a way forward in the midst of pain. Powerful."

—Amy Purdy, athlete and *New York Times* bestselling author of *On My Own Two Feet*

"All I have to say is get ready. Get ready to be equipped, stripped, encouraged, and seen. Get ready to see yourself fully as you read about Ashley's journey with seeing herself. Get ready to face your pain honestly and beautifully. In this honest, beautiful, and raw telling of her story, her rising and her falling, Ashley has given us all the words we need to trudge out of the mess and find beauty at the end of it. You will sigh. You will cry, and like I, will walk away with a resounding 'I got this. I am enough. This pain will not define me.' *I Am Here* is both the anthem and the whisper of 'get back up' that everyone will find an exhale at the end of. Get ready."

—Arielle Estoria, poet, speaker, and author

"*I Am Here* is a must read! Ashley has taken life's darkest moments and transformed them into an honest and wisdom-packed guide for us all to quit living in fear and start living the life we've always dreamed!"

—Desiree Hartsock Siegfried, host of the *Heart of Purpose* podcast

"If Ashley just wrote words, she'd be an incredible writer. If she just told stories, they'd be compelling. If she spoke to you, you'd feel like she saw you from the inside out. But Ashley is more than words and stories . . . she pours herself into cracking her soul open in order to help others heal, grow, and thrive."

—Jasmine Starr, photographer, brand strategist, and entrepreneur

I AM HERE

Ashley LeMieux

The Journey from Fear to Freedom

HarperOne

An Imprint of HarperCollinsPublishers

HarperCollins books may be purchased for educational, business, or sales promotional use. For information, please email the Special Markets Department at SPsales@harpercollins.com.

FIRST HARPERCOLLINS PAPERBACK EDITION PUBLISHED IN 2022

Library of Congress Cataloging-in-Publication Data is available upon request.

ISBN 978-0-06-321425-5

22 23 24 25 26   LSC   10 9 8 7 6 5 4 3 2 1

For my mom and dad, who taught me how to
use my own voice and never tried to quiet it

Contents

PART 3

Reclaim Your Power

All I wanted to do was run.

After a long court battle that spanned most of our late twenties, the children my husband, Mike, and I had been raising as our own were returned to their biological family. Home was empty without them, life was empty without them, and distance seemed like the only respite. We booked a flight to Italy three weeks after they left us. I was insistent that we go, sure that the farther I went, the faster I went, the less pain I would feel.

I believed a lie: If I was moving, I was moving forward. If I was going, I was growing. I believed that I could and should outrun my pain, but by refusing to feel it, all I was doing was running in place.

Three days into our trip, I sat down in the middle of a square in Florence and found myself next to a mom and her daughter. They were eating chocolate eclairs from the same bakery that Mike and I had already stopped at several times over the course of the previous days. The smell of the dough and sugar made it impossible to ever pass it by. It was spring, so all the shop doors were wide open, the air was brisk, and the sun invited us to stay outside until it got dark. The cobblestone streets felt like someone had put us right into the middle of a movie scene, and I had been doing my best to soak it all in. I was brought back to reality when suddenly the little girl shrieked. In her tiny palm she held a tooth the size of a sesame seed. Obviously, the first she had lost. They giggled and hugged and twirled.

I'd lived that moment with my own daughter, and I watched them knowing I would never live another moment with my daughter like it again. The memory hit hard and my stomach lurched. I didn't want to be in that moment anymore; I wanted to escape. I got up and sprinted down crumbling alleyways shaded by clotheslines and past terrazzos filled with packs of tourists eating gobs of gelato. I dodged scooters and sightseers. I got lost. That day, I finally realized that pain is something you can't outrun. No matter how fast or far I went, I wasn't really moving forward. I was stuck. And I had been stuck for a long time.

The feeling accompanied me wherever I went, even if my body kept moving. It hung like an invisible cage over me, as if I were in a maze without a real way out. I felt confused and powerless. I'd stopped trusting myself to make decisions, wondering if I was actually going anywhere, and if I was, if I even wanted to be there. I felt bruised from banging my body against the same brick wall of pain, not knowing how to get my life around the immovable force that had me trapped. Feeling stuck is the torment of unlived dreams, unanswered prayers, and a deeper underlying fear that life will stay that way forever.

Right outside the Duomo, I stopped. With tears running down my puffy cheeks and sweat dripping down my back, I threw my hands up in the air and screamed to the city, "I am here! I am right here!"

I heard my own voice ricochet off the old stone building and for the first time in ages, I felt its power. It alarmed me at first. I hadn't heard my voice for so long, and I was uncertain if I was even allowed to feel the newfound strength that was tingling throughout my body. I'd forgotten about the girl buried inside of me who was so full of life, and I was surprised that she was still in there. I decided to test it again, and yelled, from the deepest part of my belly with my hands straight up to the sky, "I am here! I am right here!"

Today I believe that those words, shouted aloud in that moment, surrounded by the pigeons and street musicians and fountain spray, saved my life. That patch of sidewalk was where I went from stuck to actually stepping forward into freedom. And I believe that today, with this book as a guide, you can step forward too.

As I've worked with women over the years, I've seen how stuck can look like something as seemingly small as life taking an unexpected turn to the pain of grief and loss. Sometimes we get tripped up by not knowing what we want to do next in our lives, and other times by larger circumstances beyond our control. Whether you've been stuck for a day or a year, I want to help you take the first step toward getting unstuck, to find your own moment of realization and ability to shout: "I am here!"

∾

Before we get started, I need you to understand a few things about the work we're about to do.

First, if you're searching for an easy way out, this book isn't for you. Not yet anyway. The work that we're about to do together isn't about escaping your pain, it's about embracing it. There is no easy, pain-free magic spell that simply takes us from where we are and plops us down right where we want to be. If that were the case, I'd be sitting in Disneyland right now with caramel apple dripping from my face, while my kids sit next to me inhaling their ice cream, squealing about the next ride. I'm not here to show you a way *out* of your life; I'm here to show you a way *into* it, and, my friend, the terrain ahead is as rough as it is beautiful.

Second, I'm not the expert on your life. You are. What I want is to help you believe that. I'll be your guide, your cheering section, a fellow traveler even, but this is your journey. You need *you*.

Last, you are not alone. I am here with you. Throughout the course of my own healing, I learned that there are thousands of us navigating these same feelings of self-doubt, frustration, and hopelessness. You're not the only one, so set down that shame and know that you are exactly the person for whom I wrote these words. You are in the right place and I am honored to be here with you, to teach you, and to watch you walk forward out of pain and despair and into triumph, hope, and clarity. You could use a little victory right now in your life. If you don't believe you can have a win anymore, stick with me. You will believe it by the end of our time together.

In the pages that follow, I'll share my journey toward clarity and freedom to aid you in creating a meaningful life. I'll show how I created forward movement in my life using three key strategies: reframing thoughts, reimagining the future, and reclaiming power.

Reframing thoughts has become one of my greatest advantages in getting unstuck and is what we will explore in the first section of the book. I have learned that often the feelings of fear, anger, failure, and the desperation to let go are actually feelings that can serve us if we get to the root of why we are really experiencing them. Reframing thoughts is the first step to creating a powerful present and opens up the possibility of a new future.

Next, I want to give you some practical tools that will

help you find a way out of feeling trapped in whatever circumstances have brought you here. In the second section, I'll introduce you to my most powerful planning tool, the Clarity Map. That's right, I'm not just giving you a metaphorical map! Toward the middle of the book you might want to keep a pen and paper handy. Clarity Mapping is a simple, essential brainstorming practice designed to help you determine your goals, break them down into clear, actionable steps, move toward them, and sustain that forward momentum. I use it to make every large and small decision in my life, and it's the single most useful tool I implement with my coaching clients. Clarity Mapping can be like a trusted friend who redirects me back to the one resource that I always need to feel fulfillment and purpose: *myself*.

Armed with a new way of thinking that frees you from the past and a map to creating a life you love, you will be prepared to finally reclaim your power in the final section of this book. I'll walk alongside you as you declare who you are using seven bold affirmations, uncovering a newfound love and commitment to yourself. My hope is that when you put down this book, you will walk forward toward your future with confidence.

Why me? To start, I've had to do this work myself. I wrote a little about that experience in my first book, *Born to Shine*. The work felt hard and unforgiving at times and was often lonely. When I realized how many women feel lonely on the path to healing, I committed myself to sharing all I've learned with women like you, women who need a trusted plan to love life again. *Born to Shine* was written so that you'd give yourself permission to find light and hope, even in the darkest moments of your life, and *I Am Here* is the next step that will guide you in using the pain or frustration of your past to regenerate your current power to find more clarity, strength, and alignment than you've ever had before.

In my work with clients, speakers, and online thought leaders, I've helped women create a clear path forward in lives that once felt overwhelming, like they were lost in the weeds. Many of my clients tell me that we got more done in four weeks together than they ever could have accomplished in an entire year. I've learned where to focus the attention in life, so that we can feel freedom in the areas that once felt like burdens and become our very truest selves.

Right now, you have two options. The first option is to set this book down and keep running in the same circle, feeling confused and stuck. I know that sometimes this choice feels easier, but I promise you in the long run, it's not. When you look back, I don't want you to regret not taking the chance to live your life to the truest extent possible. Living in pain and running ragged is more exhausting than the alternative. Which brings me to your second option: to trust me, and to begin to trust yourself. Allow just an ounce of belief to settle in your body and decide that today you will start moving toward a new destination.

If you're still a little nervous or skeptical that this will actually work for you, let's start here:

Breathe in. Exhale. Make this proclamation: "I am here. I am here in my life, exactly as it is. I give myself permission to stop running. I give myself permission to be here, and I accept a bright, fulfilling, and powerful future. I am safe to be here, and to dream again."

Good. Now, say it again.

Acknowledge the power in those words.

You just took your first step. You were made for this. It's your time. You deserve to uncover clarity, confidence, and joy.

PART ONE

Reframe

YOUR

Thoughts

Why Am I Stuck?

I spent most of the past five years asking myself this question, struggling with it daily, trying to wrestle it to the ground. Some days I felt like I was on a hamster wheel, running as fast as I could but getting nowhere. Other days, it was more like quicksand, a sludge that stuck to every inch of me and pulled me downward. I was too exhausted and frustrated to even bother clawing my way out. So instead, I sat and I waited. I prayed and I pouted. Every day I believed in my*self* a little bit less and believed more in the limiting stories I'd been telling myself:

1   You're scared.
2   You're angry.
3   You're selfish.
4   You need to let go.

It was true that I didn't know where I was headed, but the biggest problem of all was that I didn't have faith in my ability to get *anywhere*.

I Am Here

There are lots of things that prevent us from taking that next step: difficult experiences; negative people; heck, even bad weather, but I believe negative thoughts may do the most damage. Fear, anger, envy, regret . . . they all cause us to feel shame, and nothing will stop you in your tracks like shame.

Shame looks a little different for everyone. For me, it's a feeling of unworthiness, the absence of hope, disappointment in who I am, and it creates a pit of despair that feels impossible to climb out of. It can be so powerful that some days, I even feel shame about feeling shame! But, sister, what if there's nothing to be ashamed of? What if our paralyzing, negative emotions are actually rooted in empowering, positive ones? What if the pain we feel is actually a product of profound love? What if the very things we are afraid of, that are holding us back, are the same things that can propel us forward into a life that feels full and free? And what if our job is to reframe these negative thoughts and emotions into the positive truths that lie beneath?

I've received thousands of messages from women around the world all trying to pin down an answer to the same questions: How do I move forward? Why am I stuck? How do I start to heal? I imagine you've found yourself in this place at times, too. Maybe you're even there now.

I'm going to share with you what I shared with them: you aren't stuck, you never have been. I know it feels like you are, which is why I want to make that extra clear: you aren't *actually* stuck. But if you don't believe you can move forward toward the life you want, you're not going anywhere. *I* sure wasn't. I was chained to my past so tightly that the normalcy of it pulling me back felt like business as usual. So let's learn to believe again and do it together.

Before I could take my first steps forward, I needed to restore faith in myself, set down shame, stop the stories, and start seeking truth. I needed to reframe my thoughts. Later, I'm going to walk you through the Clarity Mapping tool that has made a huge difference in my life, that has helped me move forward and sustain that momentum.

But before we can start drawing the map, we have to lay the foundation. In this section, I'm going to show you how to reframe your thoughts. By uncovering the positive roots of my negative emotions, I was empowered to reimagine my future, and the same can be true for you. This is your first step, your next right step, and it might be one of the biggest steps you've taken in a while. Let's get going, together.

1

WHAT IF IT'S NOT
Powerlessness?

WHAT IF IT'S
Bravery?

It has always been important to me to be open, honest, and vulnerable with the women I'm connected with. If you know me or have followed me for any time at all, I hope you trust me to tell you the truth, no matter how hard, messy, or uncomfortable it may be. And still, in all the areas of my life that I have healed and found freedom in, in all the vulnerability that has connected me to millions of women around the world, there is one truth that I just could not touch. To be honest, I had every intention of taking this story to my grave with me. Yet as I worked on the final edits for this book, it weighed heavily on me that I couldn't fully aid you in uncovering the truth and power in your life if I refused to fully uncover my own. I need to tell you that this chapter contains sexual abuse memories that could be triggering. It is okay for you to skip this chapter, or read it somewhere you feel safe, or have someone you trust paraphrase it for you. Whatever choice feels right for you is the one I am supporting you to make. And if you choose to skip ahead, I will see you in chapter 2!

∾

A few weeks ago, after years of therapy, self-reflection, and internal battle that prepared and led me to this moment, I called my mom. It was time to tell her the very thing that I have withheld from her since I was a little girl. I couldn't protect her or my dad from the pain of it anymore, because having it buried inside of me has left me feeling powerless and voiceless for decades.

"Mom, as you know, I've been in therapy since I was eighteen. I've discussed a lot of things with my therapist over the years, and you know about most of them, but there is one thing that I've been too ashamed to tell you. I've been too ashamed to tell anyone, actually. But I don't want to feel like I'm holding on to a dark secret anymore.

I don't want to feel like it's controlling my life anymore, I want my power back."

I took a breath.

"Do you remember when I was seven years old, and you asked me if my Sunday school teacher had ever touched me inappropriately? What do you remember about that day?"

My mom took a deep breath as my shaky voice stumbled over my words; I heard her inhale and exhale over the speaker. I was about to break her heart, and she knew it. "Yes. I had gotten a call that a couple of girls in your class told their parents that they had been molested during class. Your dad and I were beside ourselves. I took you on a walk around the park and told you that the bad man was now in jail, explained to you how brave the girls were for speaking out, and asked you if he had touched you, too. You were adamant that you had no idea what I was talking about. You told me it had not happened to you. When we got home from our walk I went in to tell your father. He was sobbing about the thought that his little girl had been violated, and I remember him telling me how relief washed over him as I told him that you were positive your teacher had not touched you. I've never been able to let go of that experience."

Now it was my turn to take a deep inhale. My therapist had been working with me for a very long time to help me find my power in a situation that had left me feeling powerless since I was barely five years old, when the abuse happened. One of my first memories is sitting in a church classroom in a light blue dress with white ruffles sewn delicately at the bottom, and shiny black shoes that I got to pick out for my birthday. I was quiet, as (I thought) good girls in class were supposed to be, wondering why I felt so uncomfortable sitting on the lap of a man who was supposed to be teaching me about Jesus. Wondering why my stomach would feel like it was going to throw up even though I loved the Cap'n Crunch my dad let me have that day for breakfast. I remember feeling that it was all really confusing.

I hate that I still remember the weird, stinky way he smelled. Like sweat and pepper, and sometimes it was so strong that it made me go dizzy. The kids who were in the class with me were afraid, just like I was. We never said we were afraid, because we didn't know what we were afraid of, but I could see the fear in their big, round eyes as we'd all line up at the beginning of class, hoping that we were not the one chosen that day. How they looked on the outside is how I felt on my insides. On the Sundays where I was chosen from the small classroom lineup, sometimes there was also relief that it wouldn't be anyone else, that the rest of the girls in my class wouldn't have to be so afraid that day.

My voice choked with emotion. "Mom. I've been too ashamed, too embarrassed, too worried about hurting you and Dad my whole life, to be able to tell you the truth. I didn't know how to tell you when I was a kid. I was embarrassed, I didn't want to break your hearts, and I was afraid what you would think about me. But the truth is, that man molested me, too."

There it was. My truth was living outside of me for the first time in twenty-eight years. The truth that had driven a wedge between the world and how I viewed myself. The truth that had distorted the value that I thought I had, the truth that has given me night terrors even to this day and made me wet the bed until I was an embarrassing age. The truth that made me act quiet and shy, not believing my voice was important. The truth that led me to deeply question religion and God and feel shame about intimacy and womanhood for my entire life. The truth had finally been set free. And now I felt like I wasn't carrying all the weight anymore.

I didn't know how my mom was going to respond. I know from my experience and from what I've heard from other women how experiencing sexual abuse can make you wonder if the people around you are going to believe you. If they're going to look at you differently, tell you how you were wrong not to stop the abuse. Sometimes it just feels like it would be easier for everyone to keep it to themselves.

A moment later, my mom spoke, her voice loving and warm, "Ashley, I am so sorry. I can't believe you have had to carry this alone for all these years. I am so sorry I didn't know. I am so sad that I couldn't protect you. I've never been able to let that experience go. Something about it kept coming back up, and now I wish I would have done better at helping you."

I could feel the relief flood my body, and we talked for an hour. She asked me questions about how I have handled it, if it impacted other things in my life. And then, with every word I needed to hear, my mother told me that I had nothing to be ashamed of or embarrassed about, that she would support me if I chose to tell my story, and that I hadn't done anything wrong.

I finally took a breath after what felt like a very long time. She wasn't angry at me for lying to her, she didn't think I was broken or shameful; all she had was so much love that it lit up dark places I had been trying to keep buried. I am so grateful for her loving response. Before she hung up, she asked me if I'd like her to tell my dad. I knew his heart would shatter, and I told her I would like to talk to him after but would appreciate her telling him first. I love my dad, and I couldn't carry the weight of breaking his heart, too.

It has taken many years and a lot of therapy, and it has been one of the hardest things I've ever had to work through, but as I accept this deep truth about my life—that I was molested at the age of five, and that over a year later another girl in my class finally came forward to create an investigation that would lead the abuser to be caught—I can say that I now feel brave. I look back on who I was as a child, struggling to understand what was happening, feeling anxious and alone, and still finding the bravery to show up in a world that terrified me. The shame that has followed me in the shadows since I was an innocent little girl doesn't have to be buried inside me any longer. I have nothing to be ashamed of. I did nothing to deserve the abuse, and the burden of guilt for any part of it does not lay on me. My voice wasn't able to stop something that felt so, so horrific, and that is not my fault. I can also let go of the shame I felt around not being the one to use my voice to tell my parents or authorities—I have compassion for that little girl who was managing the best she knew how. That is not mine to carry.

I've felt powerless many times in my life, but it all stems back to this memory, this moment in time where an older man abused his power to try to take mine away. And it has taken me over two decades to finally find truth in a new story—that my power is actually what has kept me here. That nobody is strong enough to take it from me. The inner bravery to keep pressing forward, to keep believing in goodness and light, to keep reaching for love and joy, is a power that cannot be manipulated by anyone else for their own gain. That power is mine. And the strength I had to tap into it at a very young age is something I am now proud of.

Whatever your story looks like, you've probably felt

powerless at times in your life, too. I know that it feels easier to fast-forward and bury those stories that make us feel like a victim, where we have no control. Have you told yourself that you are powerless? Maybe you've never verbalized those words, but have you acted like it? Have you internalized shame, have you stayed quiet, have you lived out of fear? What I had to learn was that just because I felt powerless didn't mean that I was. I needed to reframe how I thought about who I was, what I had experienced, and the lasting effect it had on my life. I needed to reframe the truth for myself: What if we are filled with so much power that not only have we survived the worst moments of our lives so far, we've become triumphant over them? We've all held on, pressed forward, and risen up to meet challenges that we never saw coming, that nobody ever gave us a road map to show us how to handle. And yet, we've done it. *You've* done it. Because you are strong. And because you are so beautifully brave.

It took me years to grow to a place of wholeness after experiencing the feeling of powerlessness that stemmed from abuse I endured as a vulnerable, young child. Years from the elementary student who was too afraid to raise her hand to ask to go to the bathroom to becoming the woman who finds bravery in her voice and gives herself permission to express the inner truths of her heart. I handed my power over to conforming to what I thought I should be doing, to being a good girl, and now I know that being good and being powerless aren't supposed to be the same. If you have believed anything like that about yourself, I hope that reframing that belief can offer you some freedom as well.

I have uncovered bravery in my life by learning these three important truths:

1 **Your deepest power lies in being good to yourself.** Some of the first things we are taught as kids (especially as girls) is how to be kind to others, how important it is to listen to authority, to raise our hand before we speak, and how to fit into certain roles in the home and society so that we can be "good." What I finally learned was that being good doesn't mean we give our power away to other people and shove ourselves into a box to stay out of the way. Being good means that we find freedom in becoming the truest version of ourselves, as that is the only way to fully unlock our power. When you are good to yourself, you give voice to your intuition, you allow yourself to trust your feelings and desires, and you give yourself permission to advocate for your needs.

And when we are truly good to ourselves, we are good to others, too. We have it backward, that being self-sacrificing and quiet serves everyone around us. In reality, the people around you need *you*. The truest you. And that starts with being good to yourself. Bravery is found when you show up in this scary world as your true self.

2 **Powerlessness often comes from feeling afraid to voice our needs.** Feeling powerless often leads to feeling helpless. To combat this, I daily practice trusting my own voice and needs. Sometimes I have to start by asking myself what it is that I need. Then I allow my needs to become important and create boundaries with other people. It's easy to think that voicing needs and boundaries might hurt someone's feelings, but a boundary is actually the greatest way to create a thriving relationship. Those who value you and your needs will respect your boundaries.

As an example, I have identified that one of my needs is having dinner with my husband each night. When work creeps into our mealtime, I start harboring resentment toward the work we do. I was able to voice this need to Mike, and together we've identified it as an important boundary to set around our time and now look forward to spending that time together.

3 **Living out of your power, even when it feels threatened, is one of the biggest acts of bravery you can make.** I am often told that if I choose to wear a certain thing, or voice my opinion about a hot topic, or just exist that I will solicit unwanted negative comments, actions, or thoughts toward me. That if I stay quiet, small, and unseen, then I wouldn't have to worry about the harsh actions and words others make in my life. It's easy to want to stay small to avoid this confrontation. We see this verbal abuse and revictimization in sexual assault cases, where women are blamed for wearing or saying something they "shouldn't have," thus "inviting" unwanted acts against them. I am so sorry if you have ever been made to feel like you have brought any unwanted attention or cruel actions into your life. Hear this clearly: the actions of others have nothing to do with you. Those who are hungry for power, who use control to gain more, will make it seem like it is your fault because you stepped out of line with what they wanted. It is *not* your fault.

It's not easy, but the way I have learned to move past this is to practice viewing the negative energy that others try to put onto me as their own journey through pain. I think to myself, *How sad that your life has given you this lens in which you view the world. Peace be with you as you go on your way.* Being able to observe others' mean actions instead of taking on their need for control over me allows me to retain my own power, and not have it be muffled or choked out by someone else's need to steal my light. Holding on to your power is one of the biggest acts of bravery you can make.

We've started by jumping into the deep end here, so let's come to the surface for a breath. Let's end this chapter together by saying out loud (yes, I'm going to make you use your voice to speak truth into your life throughout our time together, so get used to talking out loud!):

I have permission to be powerful.
My power is good. I am not powerless.
I bring my power back from the things and
people I have given it to, and I allow my
power and my bravery to serve my life.

2

WHAT IF IT'S NOT *Fear?*

WHAT IF IT'S *Love?*

I'm going to be blunt, Ashley. You are self-sabotaging. You need to stop living in fear."

Lying on the table, I hated that the acupressurist recognized what I had been trying to hide for so long. My husband, Mike, and I had just moved to Nashville from Phoenix. Our children had been gone for an excruciating thirteen months and I was barely holding it together. I had night terrors and panic attacks. I pulled away from old friends who asked how I was doing. I developed a weird relationship with food that would trick me into thinking I was in control of something. I stayed up late so I could sleep through the morning and miss as much of my day as possible. I needed help. I'd already tried doctors and therapy groups and medication for depression and anxiety. Nothing seemed to be helping, so I decided to try acupressure after a friend suggested it.

I'll admit, acupressure was a little wild for me. When it comes to healing, I'm more into the Netflix binge and chocolate chip cookie approach than Tibetan singing bowls and pressure points, but traditional hadn't been working for me, and I was desperate. Also, I'd watched every season of *The Office* four times at this point.

It had taken six months to get an appointment with this well-known natural healer who I learned was a rare, ethereal human who stayed away from the internet, cell phones, or anything that would pull her energy away from the source of love and peace she carried with her.

Leading up to the appointment, I was excited and hopeful and curious; I felt like I was ready to come back to life. But when I woke up that morning, my stomach hurt and I felt dizzy. I got stuck on a phone call that I didn't want to take and afterward felt a little off-balance. I was obsessive over leaving on time, and even checked my planner when I went to bed the night before to triple-check that I got the time right. Despite all my careful preparation, somehow

I still arrived late, and when I showed up on her door-step, she told me I was an hour late and had missed my appointment. I burst into tears, explaining that I needed help, begging that I'd do anything, I couldn't wait months longer for another opening. She lovingly hugged me and sent me on my way, slipping a small turquoise rock into my hand. She told me I could hold on to it until our re-scheduled appointment. I may have begged for her to take pity on me, but in my core, I was relieved. I wasn't ready to confront the fear, and my whole body knew it.

Two months later I showed up for our appointment on time. She led me into a small, white room, full of oils and purple flowers and wall hangings with words in languages I'd never even seen before. I didn't know what to expect, but I knew I needed to be there. My body was done with drawn shades and dirty clothes. My legs had become wob-bly and my stomach was permanently in knots. I called it stress, I called it an ulcer, I called it a pinched nerve, I called it nearly everything except what it was: fear. I couldn't even say it out loud. But she could.

I sat on a stool in the corner of the room, immediately folding my arms over my stomach and crossing one leg over the other. I was feeling exposed, and it made me want to shrink as small as possible and protect myself. The practi-tioner noticed the way I sat, curling my body in on itself, and asked me why I didn't feel safe. She asked if I trusted her enough to loosen my arms that locked tightly over my stomach and put both my feet on the ground. I was living in true fight-or-flight mode, and my stomach had taken hits for so long that it became a natural reaction for me to protect it. I also felt so ungrounded in my life that I quite literally wouldn't allow my feet to sink into the floor.

Out of the corner of my eye, I noticed a rainbow crayon drawing hanging on the door. I imagined it could have been from her daughter. It sparked a feeling of safety and calmness inside of me, and the second I noticed that feeling creeping in, I immediately pushed it away, a knee-jerk reaction to feeling too vulnerable when something good came my way, even something as innocent as a drawing of a rainbow. Once I noticed the tightening in my chest and the quickness of my breath, I went all in on putting a stop to the emotions the rainbow dredged up, attacking my need to be small in the corner.

She turned and started mixing some essential oils together. She pulled out a small tissue and folded it five times into a little square. She sprinkled citrus, rose, and a splash of cedarwood onto the tissue, and then passed it to me. "How does that smell? Does it make you feel safer or is it too strong?"

I have a strong sense of smell, to the point where faint scents will make me nauseous or trigger my allergies, but I had never equated scents with something that can make you feel safe. As I took a gentle sniff of whatever potion she placed on that tissue, the craziest thing happened. I felt my body start calming down. My breath began so slow, the smell of the citrus made me feel light and peaceful, and the smell of the cedarwood brought my thoughts back into the moment. I looked at her and told her I felt like I was right where I was supposed to be.

Later, when she told me I needed to stop self-sabotaging and letting fear guide my life, I knew she was right. I was afraid to process what I had been through. I was afraid to relive emotions that I once thought were going to literally kill me, and I was terrified of accepting my pain, so I buried the emotions. The emotions had driven me into such a deep depression that I literally felt physical pain inside of my body that had made it hard to get out of bed. The anxiety that overtook me made it feel like a tropical storm was raging inside of my gut at all times of the day. I visited doctors but nothing could make me better. Underneath the heartache and fear sat the ugly truth: my children were gone.

No, I thought to myself. *No, I won't let it be true.*

At the end of the session, I grabbed my jacket and sat back on the stool in the corner for a moment. I didn't know how to comprehend the feelings she had just walked me through, so I just sat. My inner self had been exposed for the past hour, and it had felt terrifying yet liberating at the same time. As I sat, I noticed my legs were crossed and off the ground again, and my arms were folded over my chest, covering my stomach. I now noticed it was a pattern that I had grown used to living in. Fear was familiar. If you live in fear long enough, it becomes a prison, secure yes, but also filled with torment. Here's the thing about fear: it doesn't allow you to break the cycle and continue forward on your journey. Fear keeps you stuck.

On the way home from my session, I saw a little girl about my daughter's age crossing the street after school. Her backpack was too big and her smile took up most of her face. I pulled my car over to the side of the road and clenched my eyes shut. I couldn't bear to look at her skipping along the sidewalk. I was overcome with fear. Fear that I'd never see my little girl again, fear that she wasn't okay, fear that I failed as her mom, fear that she would have been better off without me, and fear that maybe everyone would have been better off without me. I started spiraling into thoughts of despair and with each new lie I told myself, the knots in my stomach got tighter and tighter.

"NO! NO! NO!" I slammed my hands against the steering wheel.

Then I remembered what the acupressurist had said about letting fear drive my life, and it all made sense. Slowly, I opened my eyes.

As I sat alone in my car, my white knuckles gripping the steering wheel, I finally allowed myself to go deeper than the fear. I wanted to figure out what was at the core of my fear, why it was playing such a strong role in my life, and why I was allowing it to make every decision for me. As I asked myself where the fear was coming from, I was surprised at the answer that I dug up.

At first my answers were surface level. I was afraid of pain, of loneliness, of feeling trapped in a life that I didn't want. Each time a new fear came up, I challenged myself to go a bit deeper, trying to understand what was bringing up so many emotions. I was afraid, but what I realized was that really, at the core of that fear, was profound love. I love my children with an intensity I could feel in every bone in my body, which made the pain of losing them become a physical pain that was equally intense. Love was at the core of my fear, but I had masked it over to try to keep my heart from shattering any more than it already had. Of course I was afraid, of course I was trying to protect myself, but in doing so, bit by bit I was forgetting about the love that drove me. And that love, even from a distance, was the most beautiful thing I'd ever seen.

I took a deep breath and let myself look at the joyful little girl. I let myself remember taking my daughter to school on the first day. I let myself relive the excitement she had as she learned how to read, the way she glowed with joy when she showed off her scribbly school projects. I even remembered the words to stories she made up about her favorite make-believe bunny. Suddenly, instead of fear, I was overcome by love. A love bigger and broader than time or space, a love that couldn't be diminished, a love that nobody could ever take away from me.

The day I learned how to reframe my fear and understand it was really love was the day my life shifted. Underneath our fears, the things we run from, are the things we love, the things we hold close and dear. Not only is it okay to be afraid, it means that you have something in your life so precious that you're compelled to protect it. If we learn to look deeper, toward the love that drives our fear, maybe fear doesn't have to be so scary. That's why there's so much power in reframing how we think about the things we fear.

Let's pause for a moment and define fear, so that together we can work through it, and uncover the good stuff that's waiting for us! Here is my definition of fear:

Fear is the darkness that warns you of danger, but it can muddy the truth of your life when it tricks you into believing that you should even be afraid of the light. It drains you and makes you feel like you can't move one more step forward.

Fear in itself isn't bad; it's often a warning light, alerting you of something that perhaps you should be cautious of. But like most things, too much of it can be harmful, can be limiting, and can draw you further away from what you love.

Speaking of love, let's go ahead and define that, too.

Love is the palpable energy of light and acceptance that makes your soul swell up and connects you to a larger power that is bigger than yourself. It sustains you, even if everything else were to be taken away. It's the light that propels us forward and reminds us about the truth of who we are.

See? A close relationship exists between the two. They both serve to remind us of where we belong, who we can trust, and what has been created for us. One prevents forward progression, while the other propels it. Usually, we are compelled to make decisions based on two things, fear or love. They are opposite, yet play a role in each other's existence.

So, what do you do when you're afraid? How do you avoid getting lost in it? How do you remember that underneath it all is that glorious, inextinguishable LOVE? When I start to feel controlled by fear, when it becomes too much of a presence, when it feels too scary, I remember these four truths:

1 **Fear is an acceptable emotion.** We will all feel fear throughout our entire lives. Sit with that for a minute. If you're ashamed or embarrassed about your fears, release that weight. Fear is a part of all of us. From the smallest child to the spiritual guru, every single human has walked through fear.

2 Fear is a physical response of our body trying to protect us from things it believes will cause us harm. The tightening of the stomach, the racing heart, and the panicked mind are all inner alarms that are trying to get us to pay attention to potentially rough waters ahead. And this is sometimes good! When we listen to fear's true warnings, we are able to escape from harm. You wouldn't kiss a king cobra on the mouth or touch a hot stove because you are afraid of the pain it will cause you, and for good reason.

We don't need to dismiss the fear we feel, but it's important to examine the root of why it is trying to grab our attention. When I feel my body respond physically in fear, I hug myself and say, *"Thank you for trying to protect me, but I am okay, and I don't need to be afraid right now."*

3 Fear suffocates love. Because you love your friends, your spouse, and your kids, you might feel afraid for their safety and worry for their well-being. Because you love them, fear gets triggered. But instead of generating more love, fear keeps us in the dark, because it is dark. I start my days now by saying this mantra: "Please allow love to guide my day, and make love known to me today." When I look for love, I find it everywhere, and it grows! When I look for fear, then I find fear everywhere, and it grows. We can choose to look for love.

4 **Fear is a judgment, not a reality.** Most of the time we are afraid of things that might happen, not something that has actually happened. Remembering that it's not real, even when it feels real, is important. Fear, based on false ideas that most likely won't ever happen, prevents us from embracing our full potential. Fear convinces us we have to rely on our own strength for everything and makes us forget there's a larger source of love, help, and hope that comes from the universe around us. The reality is we're never alone, which means we don't have to feel like we're doing it all on our own.

I'd encourage you to set aside some time this week and ask yourself what it is that you fear. Maybe even write it down in your journal. Then ask yourself, "What's behind that fear?" It might take some time, because it's hard to dig beneath the thing that has been keeping you afraid for so long. But when you can name the thing or person that lies beneath the fear, when you reframe it from a negative emotion that is keeping you trapped, you can release yourself from the hold fear has over you and move forward in love instead.

We can't eliminate fear entirely, but we can anchor ourselves to the truth that we can't actually lose the one thing we're all terrified of losing: love. When we anchor ourselves to love, no matter what goes on outside of us, our internal pull won't get carried too far down the current of fear. And that opens us up to moving forward in love. Say it with me:

I release my fear and welcome love to cover every inch of my world. I am enveloped in love everywhere I go, and love is the life force that sustains me. Love comes to me freely, and I freely give it to those around me.

3

WHAT IF IT'S NOT
Anger?

WHAT IF IT'S
Passion?

I remember the first time somebody called me angry. I was in college, recently married, and had gotten a job as a teacher's assistant at an inner-city high school in Phoenix. I was helping to lead a class that prepared juniors and seniors for college. I absolutely loved it; these were some of the hardest-working, most-inspiring kids I'd ever met, even though they had few resources to guide them.

One of my favorite kids was Jake. He didn't make it to class much, but when he did, he shone. He was smart and funny. He wanted to be an engineer and was obsessed with playing basketball. I worried about him graduating on time. Not because his grades weren't good enough, but because of how much school he was missing. He wasn't the type to willingly ditch class, but he was absent so much I worried about everything from his health to his home life. Sometimes he'd be preparing for an important test all week, only to miss the actual test day.

The more I got to know Jake, the more I realized the system was failing him. His family didn't have the resources to make sure that he was set up to learn, and it seemed like nobody at the school was advocating for him. One of the brightest students in my class didn't have the tools he needed to get through a school day let alone survive to college, and it made me angry.

I started asking the teachers and school administrators questions:

"Why don't the students have more resources to help them be successful in their classes?"

"Why aren't they being taken to college campuses to see future opportunities?"

"How can we help them really understand how to obtain scholarship money and create a new path for their lives?"

"Who's fixing this?!"

I took meetings with educators and local community

leaders and nonprofits, and after months of trying to fight the system, asking "who?" and trying to find somebody, anybody, to lead the charge, something shifted. I started asking a new question:

"Why not me?"

My anger fueled my passion, and I started working on figuring out a way to help some of the seniors that I had been working with to get to college.

At the time, I had a personal blog called *The Shine Project* and decided to ask these students to share their stories, their struggles, and their dreams on my blog. I asked my audience to help us raise the money to send these bright, deserving students to college. Together, in just one month's time, we raised enough money to award seven scholarships. I turned that blog into a business that not only awarded more scholarships but found a way to employ the students by making beautiful, meaningful jewelry that we sold and that kept our donors connected to the cause. All because I got a little bit angry.

When I realized that passion was just the flip side of my anger, I began to see how critical this reframe is. As women, we're so conditioned to be nurturing, mild mannered, and quiet, we forget that our voices are more valuable to this world than silence. We forget that we live in a world in which our voices, however loud, incessant, and demanding they may be, are desperately needed and still seldom heard. There is power in passion, and once we change the way we think about anger, once we let go of the negativity it brings, we're able to use it to create change. Anger can yield a myriad of positive results, including advocacy, action, awareness.

I want to help you reframe anger. I want you to embrace your emotions so you can be empowered instead of exhausted by them. I want you to ask yourself if it really is anger that has a hold of you or if it's passion waiting to be claimed. I use three strategies to shift my thinking when I find myself consumed, wanting to hit the wall instead of breaking down the barrier.

1 Identify what is actually causing the anger.

Anger, I think, is more of a response than an emotion. When I'm triggered and don't feel safe, anger feels as automatic as sneezing, but I try to take a moment, be still, and ask myself what's going on behind that response. Is it because the anger is easier to feel than the underlying pain? Is it because I'm having trouble articulating and understanding my true feelings?

Because anger so quickly leads to action, I always try to get still and dig to the root of the issues when I feel my blood beginning to boil. Sometimes I do this by concentrating on my breathing and shutting my eyes. Other times, I go on a walk or a run to burn off some negative energy and make room for positive, purposeful thoughts. You don't have to physically stop to create stillness; in fact, sometimes I can't create it at all unless I'm moving!

2 **Validate the feelings of anger and pain.** Often we run from these feelings because they feel too big and hard to face. But I want you to know it's okay to feel however you feel. You don't need to suppress anything. When you suppress anger, you also suppress passion, and your passion is exactly what this world needs. Remember, this isn't to get you *over* your anger, it's about getting *through* to it, understanding, embracing, and ultimately using it.

3 **Make it purposeful.** If something happens to cause me frustration, if I stumble upon a rude comment or bad book review, I ask, "How can this experience serve me and the greater good?" I very rarely come up empty-handed.

This question has bailed me out of more tantrums, harsh replies, and enormous Instagram diatribes (thank heavens!) than I can count. It helps me unlock my passion, and I believe it could help you unlock yours too.

Take a moment to think about something you've felt angry about, either in the past, or currently. Why do you think it makes you feel that way? What purpose might it have? Perhaps you experienced a tumultuous childhood? That might make you the perfect advocate for youth in the foster care system. Maybe you're feeling angry about environmental policy? That's a great place to start addressing sustainability in your own life, in your office, or in your community. Maybe your anger and sadness are really a positive pull from your compassion, to lead you to figure out the real reason that one kid in class never shows up. It could be the call to start showing up for them.

Is there an action you can take that is fueled by your passion about this topic?

I get flooded with messages from passionate women asking me why I am not talking about this world issue or that current crisis more. These women are like you and me, heartbroken from other people's pain, and angry that nobody is doing enough to fix it. I respond to them, "This is an absolutely heartbreaking crisis that you should feel angry about. But I cannot carry the weight of the entire world, which is why I put a lot of energy into the places that I know my anger is supposed to help bring light to. It sounds like you've found what you're passionate about, too. Your anger is calling you to get involved in this cause, and I can't wait to see what changes you make!"

Our passion is right in front of us. What are you angry

about? What do you wish more people were speaking up on? That's your passion. Let it rise and bring it to life.

If you're anything like me, you'll face critics along the way; welcome them and learn from them and the experiences they bring, but don't pander to them. Just because you're passionate about something doesn't mean that everyone else will be, and that's fine; it's not your job to worry about pleasing them. It's not your job to make sure everyone else is comfortable. If your passion makes you alive, happy, aware, and inspired, then it serves all of us, whether you're leading a huge organization or volunteering once a month, when you can, or leading your little tribe of sticky fingers at home. The role passion plays in our lives is going to look different; it's supposed to. What matters is that it's present and that you are too. I don't always practice this perfectly and you may not either. That's totally okay, but don't sweat it. You're here to work on yourself, not beat yourself up.

When you see your passion in motion, when you watch anger transform into positive action, you might realize how useful seeing red can be. Once you learn to reframe anger, you might find that a few other emotions soon follow. Becoming overwhelmed might become getting motivated and inspired. Becoming a little heartbroken by the world might be the key to making it a better place. Your biggest adversary might help you become your best advocate.

Go on, ruffle those feathers. Go on, get angry. Go on, discover your passion and let it lead the way. It's time to take action.

My anger, my passion, and my voice are important. I have permission to express my anger, my passion, and my voice. They are changing the world. I am changing the world!

4

WHAT IF IT'S NOT *Failure?*

WHAT IF IT'S *Growth?*

I've always been a writer. At eight years old, when asked what I wanted to be when I grew up, I would say, "a writer who helps people heal their hearts." (Yes, I really said that.) I would run home from school, head straight to my room to pull out my purple spiral notebook that I had labeled with my pen, "Ashley's Private Journal—Keep Out." I wrote poems and stories, and unleashed all my thoughts and feelings that I had throughout the day onto those lined pages. I was deathly shy, so my best friend was that notebook, and it kept all the things I didn't feel brave enough to say out loud. After I was done writing, I'd slide it under my bed to wait for me until the next day. In college I was an English major, writing at least ten long pages a week for various classes. Knowing I wanted to write for a living, I lived life, I journaled furiously, and I waited patiently until I felt like I had a story that was worth telling.

I always thought I would write fiction. I wanted to create stories in faraway places where people could safely escape their pain and find healing. Then came the real-life story I never wanted to tell. Nobody sharpens her pencil, cracks her knuckles, and sits down to write about the loss of her children and consequent swan dive into severe depression with a smile on her face, but I felt that if I could share my story, it could help women who might have experienced the depths of loss, grief, and depression in their own lives. I desperately wanted my pain to be used for something greater, something that would help others. I wanted to write the words that I had been searching for in my own time of pain.

Honestly, I thought the path to publication would be easier than it was. I'd been writing for years on *The Shine Project* blog, speaking at events, building an audience who I hoped would come to the book. I was lucky enough to secure a fancy literary agent who could market a winter coat to a cactus, who helped me put together a killer book proposal. I even blocked off some time in my upcoming schedule so that I could sit down and write once the inevitable book deal from the perfect publisher came through. We sent the proposal off to the nation's largest, most prestigious publishing companies and I knew my long-awaited dream was about to come true; I waited with a virgin celebration drink in my hand.

And then the rejections started rolling in. Not from one publishing house, not four, but all of them. One by one I read their various feedback: I wasn't Christian enough. The characters weren't developed enough. The writing wasn't strong enough. *I* wasn't enough.

I felt like a failure. Twenty-five times over. When I got my last rejection, I went dizzy. Instead of bringing me the paper-wrapped bouquet of flowers that I had felt I deserved, the universe hit me upside the head with a frying pan. Ooof.

Remember the anger we talked about in the last chapter? I felt every ounce of it. It burned through my soul and tightened in my chest and then burst out of my eyes in the form of giant, hot tears. I was angry at just about everyone: my agent, God, the teachers who encouraged me, the publishers who rejected me, and mostly, at myself for daring to believe in something good again. I had been a lot of things in life: a teacher, a wife, a mother, a businesswoman, but never a failure, not like this. I didn't know where to point my compass, but I resolved that I just wasn't meant to be an author. I had failed. Full stop.

Failure. It doesn't just halt you in your tracks, it sticks its leg out and trips you when you're going full tilt. Then it giggles when your pants split. And although it introduces itself to every human on this planet, when you're going through it, you feel like the only one. In the same week, some of my close friends had gotten book deals with the very publishers that had turned me down, and I was convinced that life's fiery darts were directed only at me. I sat with it, contemplating alternate career paths that ranged from game show contestant to lawyer.

As I was journaling through some of my pain one afternoon, I read the words on those private pages and knew that so many other women had secret, hidden pain, too. As much as I had wanted to be seen and supported in my own painful journey, there were millions of other women, like me, who were also desperate for support. I couldn't let twenty-five noes stop me from doing the work that I knew I was born to do. I needed to reach these women, or I was turning my back on the very message of not giving up that I was trying to get into their hands in the first place.

I decided to write my book. I committed to hiring my own editor, putting on our own book tour, and self-publishing the words that I still believed in with all my heart. It wasn't the path I had dreamed of, but hearing no from other people didn't change the importance of the words I knew could help women change their lives. My perceived failure had become my greatest learning experience.

In the eleventh hour the book got picked up by a very small publisher. What happened next is a result of not quitting. Our book tour sold out to thousands of women, and the book I convinced myself nobody wanted hit number 2 on the Barnes and Noble Bestsellers list. They weren't even carrying the physical book in more than a couple stores, so they upped the order fast. It eventually made the top 10 on Amazon's bestsellers, and even hit the Publisher's Weekly Bestsellers list! I can't even toot my own horn on this; what I've learned from the ups and downs of this process is that the book sales had nothing to do with me and everything to do with the women who loved this book so much that they bought it and shared it with their families and friends. I wrote a book that helped people heal their hearts, and I did it my way.

If I hadn't experienced failure, it would be harder for me to understand the level of disappointment and self-doubt that makes us question who we are and if we're good enough. If I hadn't experienced failure, I wouldn't be able to connect with women in the places they've fallen short, in a way that helps them keep moving forward.

Many of us have a false understanding that things in

life will happen flawlessly and effortlessly every time. And when they don't, we chalk it up as failure and allow it to stop us from dreaming anymore. But what if the reason failure stops you is to get you to pay attention to where you're going and how you're getting there? What if failure is really time and space for growth? What if we can learn to see it differently, and reframe it from a negative to a positive? When it came to publishing my book, it wasn't the universe that needed to shift; it was me.

Let's break down what failure really is and explore how it can spur incredible growth. As much as I hate to admit it, failure has taught me more than success ever could. And if you were to ask other women that you look to as examples of success, I believe they'd tell you the same thing. The people who find success in their lives aren't the ones who got it right on their first try.

It's also important to remember that people are given different privileges in life that make some people have to keep standing back up more times than others. Based on where we live, where we grew up, the color of our skin, our gender, or how we look, among other things, we are impacted by elements that we did nothing to earn or even choose. These privileges can put someone like myself further down the path than someone who was born into a different life. I admire and honor those who have had more odds against them than I have had, who were born into circumstances that didn't make it easy, and who keep getting back up, moving forward, and who have earned their success because of their work and merit.

We can't control our environment, or the messages or limitations society tells us we'll become, but we can take the destiny of our future into our hands, and fight for what it is that we want. Those who don't give up are the ones who understand that failure is an absolutely essential part of growth, because it gives us direction, keeps us innovative, and reminds us just how strong, persistent, and tenacious we can be.

When the rejections were rolling in, I started writing a new story, but it wasn't the uplifting memoir I had hoped for. It was called "Ashley LeMieux: Colossal Failure." It was filled with lies about who I was; I was basically the J. K. Rowling of negative self-talk. I know I'm not alone. Here are five big lies we tend to tell ourselves about failure, and why we need to recognize and call them out as the lies that they are:

1 **Failure is a reflection of who I am.** Failure is a thing that happens *to* you, it isn't you. So many women who have reached out to me believe they are the absolute embodiment of failure, but, sister, you can't *BE* a failure. It's an event, a result, an unfortunate but often totally necessary part of getting better, stronger, and smarter, but it isn't a part of your identity. If failure is a reflection of anything, it's your bravery, the willingness to put yourself out there even though it's scary, and that's something you should be proud of.

2 **Failure means I'm on the wrong path in my life.** This one guts me. It's like somewhere along the way we were told we will have *one* sign from the universe to make sure we're in our tidy little box, fulfilling our *one* purpose, and if any resistance comes, then it must mean we took the wrong course and need to jump ship immediately. Imagine if I took my failure to secure a book deal as a sign not to write. This next book wouldn't exist, and I would be filling my time with things that don't fulfill *me*. I have reframed my views and see failure, or even resistance, as a sign that I'm actually headed in the right direction. I don't use it as an escape route from a dream. Remember, an easy way may not be the right way. Just like you can't build up bodily strength without working out and using resistance against your muscles, it's the same for our dreams and goals.

3 **If it isn't perfect, it's a failure.** Do you believe that you should execute everything you attempt perfectly? A lot of us do. And my guess is that if you allow yourself to believe this lie, then you spend so much time trying to get it exactly right that you exhaust yourself and never start much of anything. Our measuring stick for success shouldn't be perfection. We miss the mark when we set standards for ourselves that we would never expect anyone else in our lives to hit.

Instead of aiming for perfection, what if you asked this question: "What can I learn from this experience that didn't go how I wanted it to?" The answer may be that you get up, dust yourself off, and uncover a new solution. It could lead to more experience that better prepares you for the next time you try. Stop holding yourself to a standard of perfection that's not obtainable, and instead embrace the innovation that will come from doing things a new way.

4 **My life looks different than [insert name here], so I am failing.** If I gauged my level of personal success on the number of children I have, the number of delicious meals I've cooked, or my patience, I could just lie down and chalk my life up as over! Your life isn't mine, and mine isn't yours. We can't keep score because everybody's playing a different game. One thing we can do, though, is cheer each other on and celebrate one another's success.

In the Shine Community, made up of women from all

different walks of life, I love how different yet united we are. It's inspiring to see women from all backgrounds, going after different things, but who share a love and support for one another. And that can be the case in your circles of friendships too. Giving ourselves the permission to be okay with our life looking different from our friend's or our sister's or our neighbor's gives us an opportunity to celebrate our individual gifts and step confidently into our own lives, instead of trying to live someone else's.

5   **Failure is the end.** It sounds absurd when we put it that way, right? But why else have you not started the business that has been on your heart? Or why aren't you committing to the relationship that you know is right for you? Or why haven't you moved to the city that's calling for you or dusted off the piano for the audition or called the adoption agency? Don't set yourself up for failure before you even start. Not trying doesn't keep you safe, it keeps you unfulfilled and in regret.

The saying "when one door closes, another one opens" is false. In fact, it drives me absolutely mad! It says that something just wasn't meant to be so another opportunity will magically open. Sometimes things *are* meant to be, but we need to learn a little more first! And most of the time, we are the ones who are in charge of opening another door and having the audacity to walk through it and experience the unknown.

You don't grow without failing. You don't learn without humility. Take a minute to pause and reflect on that. When have you experienced a failure that led you to something new? How could you see past failures as experiences that led to growth?

I know how impossible it feels to find the courage to try again after failing. To trust that you even have anything left to give. Taking a new step forward without knowing the certainty of the outcome after your dreams have been crushed is one of the bravest decisions you could ever make. From what I've seen happen in my own life, I'm confident that the only times we actually fail are when we let failure stop us from trying again.

The next time you fail, and find yourself facedown in the dirt, I want you to remember that I've been there and that the dirt is a dang fine place to start growing. We often shy away from getting too dirty, and we view face-planting in the mud as an embarrassment and bad reflection on who we are. But I have learned that the dirt is where we are able to grow some strong roots. And those roots help us take the storms of life without being uprooted too easily. You're not alone out there, my fellow seedling. I spend plenty of days up to my knees in that muck myself and I'm with you reaching for that sunshine. Keep reaching, keep going, nurture yourself, and remember that an epic fail might be just what you need to flourish.

*I am exactly where I need to be. I invite
growth, learning, and new experiences into my life.
Each new experience is working for me. I let go of
expectations, and trust the journey of growth that
I am on, to lead me exactly where I need to be.*

5

WHAT IF WE DON'T NEED TO
Let It Go?

WHAT IF WE NEED TO
Embrace It?

I thought writing *Born to Shine* would help me let go of my grief. Isn't that what we are always told—that freedom comes from letting go of the thing that is hurting us? Instead, it forced me to confront my grief *and* decide how I really felt about serial commas all in the same shot. I relived some of the most painful moments of my life, in detail. I had to remember the exact color of my daughter's bedroom, the number of toadstool houses in her fairy garden, the way her breath smelled sweet in the morning. Processing it all felt like I was trying to take a drink out of a fire hose. Every time I leaned in for a sip I nearly drowned.

I was desperate to let go of my past; that's what all the books and podcasts and experts told me I needed to do. I tried nearly every kind of therapy, massage, supplement, and yoga practice that promised healing, but I just couldn't seem to get there. The book was due, my heart felt more broken than ever, and I was absolutely, indisputably, stuck. I couldn't run away from my pain, I felt haunted by my past, and there was no escape.

What finally unlocked it for me was something my therapist told me one day. "Transformation has nothing to do with letting go of your past. Your past isn't broken and it's not something to run from, it's a part of who you are. Allow it to work with your present to create your future. Transformation happens between the place of no longer and not yet."

I closed my eyes and thought about my children. I realized that letting go of them wasn't a transformation I could or would ever want to make. The deepest relief settled over me as I realized, I didn't have to choose a side. Life wasn't a game in which either my past or my present prevailed. I could have both. The most beautiful truth began transforming me that day; our power comes when we embrace both our past and our future and use them to create fertile soil for our lives. Fertile soil can only sprout fruit in the present moment; it can't change a winter storm from the year before. But the winter storm can prepare the soil for new life to spring forth from again.

What if we don't need to let go to break free of what has been holding us back? What if instead, we need to go in, to the center of ourselves, and embrace our lives, the good and the bad?

Sisters, your past is a part of you, as much as the heart in your chest. It may be painful, you may not be at peace with it, but it has value. Letting it go would mean losing a part of you. What if you could look back on your past experiences with love and acceptance, so that you could uncover the power to look forward with hope?

There are a few steps that will allow you to reframe this thought so that you can make peace with your past, not letting it go, but letting it serve your present and your future. If you follow these three steps, you'll be able to uncover more power in your present life, while honoring your past and preparing for your future.

1 **Acceptance.** The act of fully receiving your life as a gift will set you free in ways that nothing else will. Acceptance brings freedom because you stop protesting or trying to force change to an event or situation in your life. You allow it, and yourself, to be. You stop trying to fight your way out, and instead, go into the

center and learn. Acceptance brings gratitude and fulfillment as you discover that your life is working for you,
not against you.

Here's what practicing acceptance looks like for me.
If I start feeling overwhelmed with my life, wishing I was
feeling differently or that things could feel easier, I start
saying out loud things I am grateful for. The gratitude I
feel creates real, tangible optimism throughout my body,
and it becomes easier to accept my life because I can feel
all the gifts it has brought me. It's easy to give a lot of
weight to hard circumstances in our lives, allowing them
to overshadow everything else, but when we focus on
giving weight to the good stuff, too, we are more capable
of accepting our life. Acceptance creates the heartbeat
of freedom to live, and enjoy, your life.

2 **Forgiveness.** I know how hard forgiveness is. Honestly, when it came to losing my kids, I never thought forgiveness would be possible. My story wasn't going to end
with everyone holding hands, and in fact, I never want to
see some of the people in my story again. So if this part
is painful for you, I understand. It's painful for me, too. I
would argue, though, that carrying around resentment,
maybe even hate, is more painful.

Who do you need to forgive? Perhaps it's a person, or
a situation, or the universe for not having your back, or
maybe you need to forgive yourself. If you're like me, it's

all of the above. Don't worry, there's hope no matter what edge of the spectrum you fall on.

Here's an exercise that I was taught. Think of the person you need to forgive and say out loud: "I send her (or him) the same love and success that I hope to bring into my own life. Please send her joy that allows her to be free and fulfilled. Fill her life with happiness and love and let her feel how loved she is."

The first time I did this, tears rolled down my face, because it was the hardest thing I had been asked to do since the day we lost my kids, and I also knew it was exactly what I needed. I repeated the words and said them for the next seven days. Over the course of the week, I felt lighter. I still have to practice forgiveness for this person and plenty of others, but I'm not held hostage to their actions. I'm free.

I encourage you to try this exercise over a few days and see how you feel. Only when we start to forgive and accept comes the freedom to move forward.

3 Gratitude. I want you to finish this chapter feeling the possibility that your past is now serving you instead of holding you back, and feeling grateful for that. Now that you've reframed how you approach failure as a way to dig your roots deeper into the soil, how can the things you've experienced in your past keep you growing up toward the sun? Let me walk you through a gratitude journaling exercise that has helped me.

Start by writing a list of things that you're grateful for in your life. At the top of your paper write: Evidence That My Past Is Serving My Present. Now, create a column and in that column, write down five experiences in your past that were hard, uncomfortable, or that keep negatively impacting you in your life. What you put on that paper belongs to you, no one else will see it.

In the next column, write a present circumstance that your past is now serving. If it doesn't click all at once, it's okay, allow it to take time and invite yourself to start looking for the ways that all the things you have been through are now serving your life. You may be great at listening because you grew up feeling alone and have become the friend you wish you always had.

Now write another. Because of my experiences with my kids in the past, I'm a freaking phenomenal auntie. Perhaps you're the coworker who is known for always keeping their word because you know what it's like to be lied to and have committed yourself to a higher way. Or maybe you're the student who is figuring out how to pay their way through school and works more hours than anyone around you because you grew up promising yourself you'd create a better life for your own future family. Notice the things that are working *for* you, and for each additional item you write down that you're happy about, I want you to recognize and accept that it's in your life because of what has happened in your past.

Working through acceptance, forgiveness, and gratitude can help you make peace with the difficult things that have happened to you in your life, honoring how they have made you into the beautiful person you are today, scars and all. By embracing that person, you will be able to move forward toward what's ahead.

As you move your life toward the feelings and emotions that you once tried to escape, you can embrace your life in a way that then gently releases you from being trapped. How to let go of the thing hurting you was never the right question. Reframe that. Embrace your life, yourself, and your feelings so they can assist you and bring the transformation that you've been searching for.

I embrace my future, and it brings me
joy and power in my present. Everything
is working out for my good.

6

WHAT IF IT'S NOT
Self-Indulgence?

WHAT IF IT'S
Self-Love?

After our kids left, the place I felt best was at work. Working kept my mind and time fully occupied, so there wasn't any time in my schedule for heartache. After weeks spent working long hours, Mike gently suggested that I take some time to reconnect with *me*. I responded with a lot excuses, but finally agreed to go on a weekend retreat in upstate New York.

Leaving wasn't easy. I had a checklist of about five thousand items I insisted on getting through before I left. I was certain that the office and my home would both buckle under the pressure of a weekend without my expert micromanagement. I was hesitant as I kissed Mike good-bye and walked through the airport doors, but he and our waggly-tailed dog, Oliver, drove away from the curb quickly with an encouraging honk and a wave. For the first time in a long time, I was alone and so terrified of the time and space I had to think and feel that I would've applied for a job with the TSA if they were hiring. The truth hit me hard. I thought all the people I was leaving behind needed me, that they were totally dependent on my guidance and encouragement, but really, I was much more dependent on them. I wanted to be able to find a sense of safety and belonging inside myself. Instead, all I felt was fear and guilt.

When I landed in New York, I picked up a rental car to drive to the retreat center. As I started the drive, my negative thoughts went into overdrive.

Who was I to take time away when everyone else was working?

Mike needed time too. Maybe he needed this more than I did?

Traveling and "me time" don't come cheap. I should've done something better, more meaningful with the money.

And finally, the hallmark of shame: *I don't deserve this.*

Mercifully, my phone rang. Something had gone wrong at a photo shoot at work and my assistant, Jennifer, was panicked. I was frustrated that I was needed to manage a situation that should never had been a situation at all. Most of all, though, I was relieved. Something had arrived to rescue me from trying to rescue myself. I pulled the car to the shoulder and got ready to take care of business.

As I did, something incredible happened. I looked out onto the most beautiful, silver-plated lake. It caught my eye as the sun hit it and little rainbow beams bounced off the water like they were putting on a dance, just for me. Jennifer's voice began to sound faraway. I had never seen anything like it before.

"Wow," I said, lowering the phone. There was no one to share this moment with, but it didn't matter. It could be just for me. I could enjoy it, revel in this one precious moment, without fear or guilt or shame. If I tried, maybe the whole weekend could be like that one perfect glance. I told Jennifer I was confident she could handle the issue at work and we could talk about it when I returned.

Then, after another good long look at the lake, I made a playlist that was exclusively *NSYNC and Britney and for the next two hours of my drive, I wiggled in my seat like I was back in high school on a Saturday night with friends. I was having fun, with my very own (it turns out) very fun self! In taking care of business, I had forgotten to take care of me. I'd lost the ability to play, imagine, and just revel in the experience of living. I'd buried myself deep, I was driven by professional accolades instead of personal growth. I was strict. I was dependent on those around me for affirmation and I kept too busy to care. It was time to allow myself to shine again, with no apology about it. I showed up to the retreat excited to be alone, to turn on Backstreet Boys at night in my room, to give myself everything I needed, that weekend and beyond.

Self-love is not self-indulgence. I want you to feel that in every part of your bones because it is time for all of us to set the record straight. It isn't optional. It isn't superfluous. It's a necessity. It's easy to give our love to others, to our partners or kids or our work. It feels good and it looks good, but you can't move forward on empty. The number one concern I hear from women who want to chase their dreams, or go on vacation, or heck, even run an errand alone, is that they feel guilty. We learned that productivity and purpose is found in the nurturing and care of other people, and for some reason we took ourselves out of the equation. Mothers become martyrs, girlfriends become doormats, and women who work become women who work too hard just to prove that they belong. You always belong, sister, just as you are, and you don't need to sacrifice your sanity, safety, happiness, or peace to succeed. I would argue that you can't succeed without some level of self-care, awareness, and nurturing. At least not for long.

If I don't hold space for myself, I start to spiral. I lose focus and my creativity gets compressed into a torture chamber of not good enough. I begin to compare myself to other women around me, and my insecurities deepen while my grace for myself lessens. When my relationship with myself suffers, it then seeps into my relationship with my husband, my family, and my employees and makes those relationships suffer too. My work starts being affected, which means the tools and content I'm creating for my online readers lose the power and impact that they otherwise could have had. I could self-sacrifice my entire life, and if I did, the best-case scenario of my life would be everything I just listed in this paragraph. I don't know about you, but for me, that's not a life I want to be living. It's not a life where I show up as my best self, full of love to give, life to live, and truth to uncover. Holding space for myself is the greatest gift I can give my life, and to those around me to serve the greater good. And making this shift from thinking of it as "self-indulgent" to "self-love" can make a huge difference.

This doesn't mean it's easy.

If you've found yourself in a situation where you feel guilty about taking care of yourself, I want to give you a simple, guilt-free guide with five tips to loving yourself. I know you might not be used to doing things for *you*, so if it helps, imagine doing these things for your young child or best friend. Take a minute to picture your daughter or son (real or imagined) walking in to see you practicing self-love. Imagine the impact it would have in the lives of your kids to have them witness the woman they love more than anything pour love back into herself. This is a gift that only you can give them, they can't learn it anywhere else. And you are worth that kind of love.

1 **Set apart at least ten minutes every morning for yourself.** We're going to start with this small number—just ten minutes—because I want you to see that you *do* have time for this, no matter how busy your schedule is. Think ahead the night before and decide when the best time would be. Is it before your kids get up? While you're eating breakfast? If you're proactive about it, it will actually happen.

And the best part is, you get to decide what you do for these precious ten minutes! Perhaps the ten minutes are spent reading or getting active. Maybe you watch the sunrise in quiet and journal your feelings. Maybe you start the book you've always wanted to write. You get to choose, because the ten minutes is all yours. By the end of the week, you will have spent seventy entire minutes on yourself! Imagine the possibilities of what that time will do in your life.

2 **Reframe your thoughts when you feel guilty.** When a guilty thought comes in that tries to bully you out of whatever self-love approach you are taking, I want you to notice that thought. Acknowledge the fact that it's there and then simply let it go. You can say, "I know I am feeling guilty for [fill in the blank] right now, but I am practicing self-love. And this self-love is incredibly important because then I will be able to [fill in the blank]."

3   **Do one thing new each week.** For my introverts or routine lovers, I know this one is hard. I can feel your anxiety from here! The new thing doesn't need to be jumping out of an airplane or getting a tattoo across your bicep. It can be small, like trying a new place to eat, or taking a drive through a different part of town, just enough to remind you how miraculous it is to sit and behold. Experiencing new things keeps me open to new people and ideas, it teaches me truths I wouldn't otherwise learn, and it keeps me in check when I start to believe that my way of doing things is the only way.

4   **Write a love letter to yourself.** I've found it to be so helpful to write letters to myself full of positive affirmations that are the opposite of the negative emotions I might be prone to feel. An affirmation is emotional support and encouragement to validate your actions and beliefs! For example, since we're on the topic of guilt, an affirmation might be, "I enjoy spending time with myself," or "I release all insecurities, fear, and guilt. I let go, and I am free." A couple more ideas could be: "I love myself, and I carry that love in all that I do," "I am worthy of love, and I accept all the love the universe has to offer me," "I am connected to a deep source of love that I do not have to earn, but is freely a part of me."

Write down the affirmations that feel good to you and stick them in places you will see. Mine are right on the wall next to my bathroom mirror, so that they are the first thing I see every morning. I also have them on my bedroom mirror, and in the center console of my car. They serve as a reminder of the truth of the life I am living and help me release negative thoughts before the untrue thoughts even arise.

Affirmations work powerfully when you look at yourself in the mirror and say them out loud, and they are also effective just looking at them and repeating them in your head. I set an alarm on my phone that goes off three times a day, and in the alarm notes I write the affirmation for how I want to feel that day. It's a great, positive disruption that I get daily, which helps get my thoughts and actions back on track to mirror how I want to feel.

It's easy to forget that it's not one big moment that creates our days and years, it's little decisions that all play in to how we think, feel, and act in our lives. The time you take to affirm yourself, your life, and the path you are on adds up and contributes to a life you want to be living.

5 **Practice self-love as a feeling.** When we think about self-care, we might think about bubble baths and eating chocolate and going shopping for a new pair of shoes. And as much as I love a good shopping trip and the thrill of a new pair of shoes or jeans that make my butt look perky and amazing, I've found that the high from buying something new wears off quickly. Self-care doesn't need to be flashy or expensive, it needs to be meaningful and restorative. Focus on things that will fill up your tank long term: journaling, time to yourself, surrounding yourself with beauty, doing a hobby that brings you joy. Bonus: if you focus on the intangible qualities of self-care, you're less likely to overindulge.

This guilt-free guide doesn't take much time out of your day to implement and it could mean the difference between burning out and shining bright. Practicing self-love is kind of like going to the gym (sometimes it *is* going to the gym!). It might take a few more reps before you see results, but the results will be beautiful. And self-love also means that your tank will be full so that when others come to you needing something, you have more to give.

Since I started investing energy back into myself, I've found I'm a better friend, a better boss, a better human. My capacity to love is deeper, I have more to give, and the desire to give is real. If you think this all feels too hard, I've got good news for you: you started your self-care journey just by opening this book. You're here right now because you love yourself, even if you might still be learning how it is you need to be loved. Give yourself some grace, and love, and take the next step in your journey knowing that you are worth every second of it.

Now that we've worked to reframe these negative thoughts into ones that serve us better, we're going to continue our journey by moving into imagining what our future could look like, and then actually filling out a map to help us get there. You are going to build your very own Clarity Map in the next section, using a practice that I uncovered and has now drastically transformed my life. Strap in, this is where we start putting what we've learned into action!

I am worthy of love. I thank my body, my heart, and my mind for always supporting me. I am full of goodness and I am proud of who I am. I have permission to love myself.

PART TWO

Reimagine

YOUR FUTURE

WITH

Clarity Mapping

In December 2018 I was struggling to get out of bed. Here I was, working hard to reframe my thoughts, to believe that I was worthy and capable of moving forward, but I didn't know *how* to do it. Beyond "forward," I didn't even know where it was I wanted to go so badly. The hardest part of navigating life after pain is deciding where to go next. It's not like anybody slips a map under your bedroom door.

One day, Mike came in around 11 a.m. and pulled me out of bed as he had done so many mornings before. The questions rattled around my mind: Where do I focus my time? What brings me joy? Where am I going? Who even am I? That morning I realized just because nobody gives you a map doesn't mean you can't draw one.

I sat down by the window. "What is my intention today?" I asked aloud. That one small question changed everything. I began starting every morning asking myself a different question, and over the next several months, I came up with a series of five questions that gave me a clear, purposeful plan for my day and, ultimately, my life. These five questions evolved into what I started calling "Clarity Mapping," a step-by-step planning practice that has allowed me to reimagine my future. Using it, I went from someone overwhelmed by life to someone overjoyed by it.

Clarity Mapping can be used in your personal or professional life. It's helped me create actionable steps that actually lead to somewhere purposeful. It has guided me in making big pivots in my business and has aided me in creating focus in my personal life. I've taught the practice to coaching clients and friends, and it's helped them, too. In fact, the Clarity Mapping process came together when one day I got a frantic call from a friend asking me to come over quickly. She wasn't one to ask for help or draw attention to herself. She was the one who had it all handled, the one you called when you were in the midst of a crisis. You better believe I dropped everything and went.

You might think she'd busted her leg or flooded her kitchen but no, she was overwhelmed. She was a mother to three wild young boys as well as being a speaker, a writer, and a podcast host. She had so much she wanted to offer to the world and her family, but she was drowning in her own ambitions. I could see how stuck she felt as she sat rigidly on the couch and explained the emotional chaos swirling around her. I had been there. So many times.

"I just want to know where I'm going!" she lamented into a pillow.

Then it hit me like the cartoon anvil from Looney Tunes. What she needed was what *I* needed, a map. I went home and put the five questions together on paper in a simple flowchart and finally saw the way they all fit together to form a big, beautiful picture. I felt clarity not just about the next twenty-four hours, but about my whole life. I shared it with my friend, which helped her get clarity about why she was afraid to move forward in her life and led her to launch a successful podcast. And now I want to share it with you.

Clarity Mapping is the pinnacle practice of this book. It's the five questions working together, one step to the next, to uncover the larger answer to how to live a meaningful life. It has changed my life, my sweet overwhelmed friend's life, and the lives of countless other women who want a simple, actionable way to identify their purpose and plot out their path. It's the simplest, most impactful mindfulness exercise I've found and you guys, it's *fun*!

Some have told me how they've started new businesses that once felt incredibly out of reach. Others have uncovered more confidence and have clearer direction on how and where they should be spending their precious time. Many have told me that Clarity Mapping has allowed them to get more done in four weeks than they normally would do in an entire year. It opens the gateway to a clear, focused mind.

We all have different stories, experiences, and events that shape our lives, but so many of the obstacles are the same.

Clarity Mapping is designed to work for anyone who feels ready to reimagine their future. In this section, I'm going to explain the five questions that make up the Clarity Map and give you the tools you need to begin the practice yourself. I ask myself the five questions daily, to bring intention to my days, and the finished Clarity Map is used to guide larger time periods in my life. The secret isn't hiding out in the world somewhere. It's buried right inside of you. I'm just here to show you how to uncover it.

As we begin, I want to remind you what a very wise mentor once told me: "Transformation is the place between no longer and not yet."

Though it is often the most difficult place to be, in midst of the struggle, you might find your truth, you might discover the depths of your courage, you could experience incredible growth. Clarity Mapping, actively and intentionally working on myself, being "in the midst," and sitting in the struggle have led me through pain to purpose. I want the same for you. It's in the middle where the magic happens and epiphanies come alive. Let's draw your map, let's imagine your future, let's take another step forward, together.

The Five Daily Questions

These are questions you will ask yourself to help identify what matters before you start moving through your day (morning works best for me). They are also the crucial foundation of Clarity Mapping, so return to this page (or copy it into your journal) as we go through the following chapters to fill these out for yourself.

What is my intention?

_____

_____

Why am I worthy?

_____

_____

Who can I serve?

_____

_____

What can I set down?

_____

_____

Who is the truest version of myself?

_____

_____

7

WHAT IS MY
Intention?

The first question revolves around naming and setting your intention, and simply put, an intention is a promise you make to yourself to be aware of your actions. Throughout the day, as dinner is catching fire on the stove, and your most draining client keeps blowing up your phone, and little bums need to be wiped, your intention will be grounding you, guiding you, and, most important, bringing you clarity. An intention illuminates the path you want to be on so that you can ensure that with every bump and twist along the way, you don't get thrown off course. It also adds the one thing that brings me the most power when I'm feeling depleted: purpose. Most people think that purpose is something you have to go find, but the truth is you can create it, and it all starts with setting an intention.

So often we focus on the things we DON'T want. We *don't* want to feel stressed, we *don't* want to be unhappy, we *don't* want to wake up and go to work, we *don't* want this, and we certainly *don't* want that. Our "Don't" lists are long. Setting an intention is about what we DO want. It took me a long time to even consider what I did want out of my life. I knew I didn't want to feel sad anymore, I knew I didn't want the stress my company was giving me, I knew I didn't want to feel so alone. But on November 28, I knew exactly what I wanted: gratitude (and cake).

It was my birthday, the big 3–1. Any celebration was hard without the kids, and since it's a double whammy so close to Thanksgiving, all I really wanted that day was to be left alone with my cake. I missed waking up to burnt breakfast in bed and homemade Happy Birthday cards from the little sticky fingers who made them. I needed to fill that void with something, anything, but nothing felt quite strong enough to take the place of that emptiness. I had been practicing my morning quiet time for an entire month. It wasn't easy (in fact, I think they should make meditation an Olympic sport), but I was doing it anyway.

On this particular day, maybe because I was officially *in* my thirties, I felt the pull of time tugging at me a bit more insistently than I had before. I thought more about the future, what I wanted it to look like, and how I was going to get there. I didn't want to keep feeling like I was living in *Groundhog Day*. You know, the movie where Bill Murray wakes up and every day keeps repeating itself? My grief and the sadness were becoming repetitious and stifling, and starting a new age felt like the day to break the cycle. One thing felt abundantly clear to me: the world was turning, the clock was ticking, and if I was really going to move forward, it was time to start.

I thought and I thought about what intention to choose on my birthday. Would staying in bed all day be appropriate? Maybe that could be my intention, but then again, I didn't want to disappoint Mike, who had left a note on my nightstand to be ready by 11 a.m. because he had a fun day planned for us. Perhaps I should just set an intention to hit all the Black Friday sales and shop my birthday away with some mega retail therapy to buy everything I didn't actually need. As I debated my birthday intention, my phone was so overblown with balloon emojis, I'm surprised it didn't float away. I could smell the special birthday breakfast Mike was cooking—bubble eggs (what I call over-medium eggs), bacon, hash browns, and toast.

"GRATITUDE!" I almost jumped off the floor as I yelled it, excited that on an overwhelming day, I had one set action to focus on.

My intention was clear:

I want to show gratitude to the ones who love me.

It felt easy and important. It gave me a concrete thought

to focus on that wasn't overwhelming, and that wouldn't drain my bank account.

That afternoon, I wrote a "thank you" to every single person who thought of me and reached out to wish me happy birthday. Every time my thoughts drifted to disappointment and how much I wished my kids were with me, I would gently pull my thoughts back to my intention and write another note of gratitude. I'd woken up that day wanting more than nothing else to be filled up with buttercream, but all day long, because I stayed connected to my intention, I was able to remember how full my soul already was. At the end of the day, I felt a sense of peace, achievement, and for the first time in a long time, excitement for the future.

Living with intention will look different for everyone, but the feeling behind it is the same: to create purposeful interactions in your life. Living with intention helps me spend time connecting with people I love, or learning something new, instead of wasting time on the internet when I feel like I have a moment of "downtime." Living with intention means I say yes to the experiences and offers that fuel my intention, and no to everything else that distracts me from it. With more thought as to how I want to spend my individual days, I'm able to feel progression toward the things that I want and be accountable to how I spend my time. Intention brings action, so that we can stop just thinking about what we wish life was bringing us, and actively pursue it.

My experience on my thirty-first birthday was so powerful that I began to set an intention every single morning. I knew that if I could focus on one thing, keep one promise to myself, the purpose I'd feel in my life could be profound. My intentions ranged from showing up to work meetings that I wished I could skip out on, and doing it as a big ball of love for the others who were in the room with me, to going to the boxing gym even if I felt tired. These intentions helped me create nonnegotiables in my life that brought a positive sense of discipline and progress that made me feel good throughout the day.

It finally felt like forward movement was actually starting to happen in my life. I began knowing what to focus on at work in order to feel fulfilled and help others find power in their lives, too. I was able to focus on my relationship with my husband and on specific places in our relationship that I wanted to strengthen. My experience with one intention a day has created a life that feels really good to be living in.

What's an intention you could set for today? I know you'll be tempted to think bigger than that (and we'll get there), but seeing how it feels to set and meet a single day's intention can be a great confidence boost. Try it out!

After getting the hang of setting daily intentions, I started to focus in on what my life's overarching intention should be. Again, it took some thought, but the foundational intention I've set for myself is "I guide women to help uncover their power." A single intention allowed me to become so intentional with how I was spending my time that everything I did had more heart and passion behind it than I ever experienced it before.

Now, whenever I make a decision, big or small, I ask myself if it lines up with this intention. Is it going to further the work I want to do in that area? Is it going to serve that group of women? The discipline of being hyperaware of how I was spending my time helped me be intentional with the twenty-four hours in the day that were given to me, and as I treated them as a gift, it felt like I was receiving more back in return.

Sometimes this looks like fully engaging with the people I am with instead of having my phone out, being halfway present and halfway trapped in a social media daze. Other times it gives me a sense of pride and accomplishment as I end my days feeling like I gave my very best to generate the outcomes I desire in my life. It turns out, life feels a lot more fulfilling when we're intentional with how we choose to live it.

Now it's time to create big victories in your life, asking one small question at a time. It is important to know that there is no limit on the amount of intentions you can set. I set one at the beginning of every year to lay a foundation that will keep me on track to bring results that I want to see. I set intentions for every project I take on, for my month, my days, and even for the Instagram posts that I create. For example, my intention for the words in this book was to write the truth of my life in a way where you could uncover more freedom in yours. Then, as I would start each day writing, my intention would be: "to replace fear and shame with deep love." Any time I would tense up because I was writing a painful part of my story, I would mindfully write from a place of love to myself. I'd picture what I would say to my daughter if it was her story and allow that love to melt away the shame and fear.

What kind of intention do you want to make? What area of your life could use some direction? This process can take as little or as long as you want and need it to, depending on what you are working on. The only rule is that you listen to your own gut! Sometimes determining your intention might be easy, you might be absolutely teeming with brilliant ideas! When I'm struggling to think of ideas, though, I focus on two things: the Aim (How do I want to feel?) and the Action (How can I create this feeling?)

The Aim

When we start with knowing and visualizing how we want to feel, it creates space for us to realize that the outcome we want is truly possible! Starting with the feeling allows us to block out the noise of everything else that is competing, and stay true to the place inside of us that is guiding us to move forward with clarity and power. When our feelings work with us, instead of against us, that is when our intention is able to become a reality because we get out of our own way.

To uncover your aim, ask yourself: "At the end of today (or this project, event, etc.), how do I want to *feel*?"

In the winter of 2018, I was starting to feel disconnected from Mike. We both had transitioned to working from home, which meant that we were literally together 24/7. There wasn't a real separation between working hours and just married-spending-time-together hours, and since we were both working on our own companies, we didn't seem to share a common goal. For so long, our goal had been just to survive in our marriage, our businesses, and our day-to-day routines, but now we were past that place and needing to keep progressing forward together.

I didn't know if Mike felt the same way, but I knew that I felt like even though I was around him all the time, I didn't feel connected. I wanted more purpose and intention inside of our relationship, so I decided that I would start focusing on it. But how? What intention could I set that would get us there?

I started with the aim: I knew that at the end of each day I wanted to *feel* that Mike and I were making forward movement together. I wanted us to share quality time, not just go through the motions of being married, but to actually feel connected. I envisioned what feeling like that would be like. It would create a stronger bond, a greater impact that we could make on the world around us together, and even add more fun into our lives! I knew these feelings were possible because we had them so many times before and we loved each other, so I committed to bringing those feelings back into our relationship.

The Action

With my aim uncovered, I now needed to put those feelings into action. I decided I needed to show up as a big ball of love to my marriage, so that we could feel more connected. I figured that if I first put the effort in myself, then movement would start to happen and Mike would reciprocate it. For that to happen, I would need to take control of my energy and create moments throughout my day where I went out of my way to make sure that Mike felt seen and loved. I also set aside time for planning a date night, so that we would have an activity outside of our house to look forward to and have fun doing together.

That week I decided that showing up as a big ball of love for Mike would mean that I would make his meals while I was making mine, so that if he was caught up in a meeting, or running late, he would have something to eat and know that I was thinking about him. (It's important to know that I hate cooking, so Mike often cooks for us.)

Another action I needed to take was to talk to Mike about my sense of feeling disconnected from him, instead of keeping him in the dark. Because I was committed to showing up as a big ball of love, I was able to talk to him from a place of love, instead of frustration, which led to one of the most life-changing conversations in our marriage.

I had asked Mike to put into his calendar a special meeting time that would take place during the workday, so that we were both as serious about it as we would be with any other meeting. We sat together in our family room, and I brought a big white poster board, with thick, black letters written in Sharpie at the top that said, "Our Relationship Intention." I explained to him that I had been feeling that we were physically together all the time, but not really *together*. I asked him how he had been feeling, and we both listened and validated each other, and then worked together to come up with a clear path forward that would bring us closer together.

We decided to set intentions as a couple, so that we could work toward a common purpose walking hand in hand along the path. Just as I had set intentions for my own days in my morning practice, we now did that as a couple. Our first intention was to limit the noise that made us feel like it was putting a wedge in between us. We decided that there were certain people, music, media, and problems that were exhausting both of us with their negative energy. Deciding to cut out the unnecessary or harmful noise in our lives meant having some hard conversations with employees and people who had been draining us for a long time, but we finally realized that appeasing them was costing our marriage and our happiness. We intentionally started making changes, together.

To uncover the action you need to take, ask yourself: *What's one action that my future self would thank me for taking today?*

Determining your aim and action will give you a starting place so you don't feel overwhelmed or confused about where to start. Don't let the details of choosing your intention trip you up. The important part is that you start and pay attention to the impact it makes in your day! As you notice the impact, you will grow in your commitment to creating a habit of setting intentions.

So let's get started with the first question in our Clarity Map, determining your intention. Get out a piece of paper and let's get going!

What Is Your Life Intention?

No pressure, but determining your intention is the entire foundation of the practice. If there's a sweaty, heavy-lifting part, this is it. I promise, though, having a clear, well-defined picture of what you want makes it all worth it in the end.

In a recent Clarity Mapping workshop I hosted, there was a woman struggling to grasp her purpose. I asked her what her intention was, the big, go-for-broke, if-I-do-one-thing-let-it-be-this-in-life goal. She wrote:

I want to declutter my home.

I let her sit with that answer for a while, but I knew that was only the tip of the iceberg. We needed to uncover *why* she wanted to declutter to discover the true objective. I waited a little bit and then I asked her, "Why do you want to have a decluttered home?"

She told me it was because she wanted a clean space for her husband and children.

"Why do you want a clean space for your husband and children?" I asked. We went through the process four more times. And finally, we got there.

Proudly, she stood up and announced, "I need to declutter my mind, so I can show up for myself, my family, and the world in the way I was created to."

She started to cry, and I hugged her. If I could have cued the buzzers and flashing lights and a confetti cannon, I totally would have. We reached the root, and the root is where growth begins.

Ladies, take a deep breath, it's time to dive in. What is *your* intention for your life?

When it comes to crafting your intention, there are no hard rules. Your purpose might look totally different from your neighbor's, your sister's, or your husband's (That's right, boys are allowed too!), and that's totally fine but try to make sure that it is:

Specific: The more focused the intention, the easier it will be to live out. For example, if you're leaning toward, "I want to be a good mother," explore what being a good mother looks like to you. Perhaps your intuition is telling you that you want to be more present in your family life? Maybe being present means less screen time for everyone or managing schedules better? Maybe less screen time means more quality time together? An example of your new intention might be:

I create an intentional family life by prioritizing our relationships and increasing the time we spend together.

Remember, if you get stuck, keep digging deep, keep asking why. Don't stop until you run out of *whys*, until all that's left is deep, inexplicable desire.

Measurable: Evaluating your progress can be difficult, which is why I always recommend starting off with a measurable goal. "I want to be a good mom" is beautiful and noble, but it doesn't give you a tangible way to assess your growth. In the revised intention above, you can easily keep track of how much time you're spending with family. You can see if progress is being made, and if it's not, you now know which part isn't working that you need to tweak or rework.

Positive: Since our intentions are often rooted in our problems, it's easy for negativity to creep in and I'm not here for it, not one bit. "I want to be a good mom" implies that you're a less-than-wonderful parent. This exercise is not meant to beat you down, it's about building you up. Just like we reframed the negative thoughts into positive ones in the first section, make sure your intention is framed positively. Again, the revised version is a positive reframing of this: *I create an intentional family life by prioritizing our relationships and increasing the time we spend together.*

Once you have your intention, put it smack-dab in the middle of a paper and draw a big box around it. Here's mine:

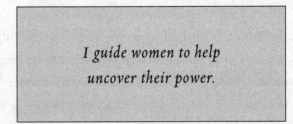

I guide women to help uncover their power.

Got your intention written into your box? Great! That's a huge first step. Everything else flows from here.

Setting intentions in my life has done everything from creating a stronger marriage to finding the right employees for my company, and heck, it's even why I am writing this book right now! When you stay focused on what you want in life, you move forward mindfully, and mindfulness is always a step in the right direction.

The next step in the Clarity Mapping process is to believe that we are worthy of good things in our lives, which can be hard for many of us to internalize. What have we done to deserve blessings? And if we get what we want, how long until the other shoe drops? As long as we sit in that mind-set, we'll never move forward, so the key is resting peacefully in the knowledge that you are truly worthy.

8

WHY AM I
Worthy?

Crying in the back seat of an Uber with snot dripping down my face wasn't one of my finer moments, but there I was nonetheless. I kept making awkward eye contact with my driver when he'd slowly pull his eyes up to the rearview mirror to check on the nutty, sobbing mess of a girl in his back seat. I kept wishing he'd say *something*, if only to liven up the soundtrack of my sniffles and gasps. I sounded like a pig trying to breathe through the mud. But he never did, so I just sat clutching my purse, snuffling my way to the airport.

Nothing bad had happened that morning. In fact, the morning was so *good* that it triggered the bizarre emotional outburst. I'd been living my life mindfully, with a daily intention and a sense of purpose. Just as I'd hoped, I began to feel myself slowly and carefully moving forward, and as I did, I became incredibly aware of my blessings: a husband who danced with me in the kitchen, a dog the size of a football who was my sworn protector, a fulfilling job, and a wonderful home. The problem was, I struggled to believe I deserved any of it. Questions I couldn't answer often kept me up at night staring into the blades of the ceiling fan.

Why me and not someone else?

Why was the world listening to me, another privileged voice, when there were so many more important people to hear from?

Why do I feel happy? Is it even okay to feel happy without the kids?

If self-sabotage were an art, you could call me Picasso (I'm working on it).

As I left the house that morning, clutching a suitcase expertly packed with the special snacks Mike sweetly packs for me when I go on trips, I began to feel a strange sense of heaviness. It surprised me. I climbed into the Uber and looked back. There, perfectly framed, flanked by two blooming planters (even the plants were thriving!) was everything I'd ever wanted: Mike grinning like a lunatic making Oliver wave his paw against his will and shouting, "We love you!" Then, another question popped into my mind:

Why do you deserve love? What makes you so special?

Before I knew it, I was crying. In a stranger's Toyota Scion.

I know plenty of women who struggle to accept the joy they have and strive for the joy that they yearn for. We ask ourselves these questions: Why me? Why do I get the baby/promotion/home that ____ doesn't get? Why should I ask for more, strive for more, when I have so much already? And often, we struggle to come up with satisfying answers so we settle for this one:

You don't deserve it.

And because we feel like we don't deserve it, we hold our breath and wait for the other shoe to drop. You might know exactly what I'm talking about when I say that sometimes joy can be the scariest emotion of all, because we know how far down we can drop if it disappears. We start preparing ourselves for it all to be taken away from us, guarding ourselves so it doesn't hurt so badly. I can't tell you the number of times amazing things have happened, only to result in me obsessing about what catastrophic doom was looming around the corner.

I got in the habit of thinking that everything had to balance out. If something great happened, it just meant that the universe was giving me a little cushion of happiness before it was all ripped away. I began to feel more comfortable living a life of pain than knowing how to accept the blessings in my life. What a sad, and exhausting, way to live.

Ladies, it is very, very difficult to create forward motion

in your life, to arrive at a place of peace and fulfillment, if you don't believe you're worthy of your position there.

So how do we believe?

As I settled into my work trip (after my Uber breakdown), I knew that I didn't want to keep being afraid of joy, and I wanted to believe that the good in my life was not attached to a diagnosis that despair was just around the corner. The next morning, after grabbing my notebook and setting my intention for my day, a new question was born:

Why am I worthy?

I had been having such a hard time feeling worthy of finding joy in my life again. I couldn't wrap my head around being able to still be worthy of a meaningful and purposeful life. I stared at the page for so long that it started to go blurry. I knew why I was loved, I knew why I should feel joy, I knew why I was grateful, but was I really worthy? I kept going.

I am worthy because I was a good mom.

I am worthy because I work hard.

I am worthy because I give love to people and serve their needs.

I am worthy because I am strong.

It felt good to look down at a page filled with perfectly reasonable answers, but none of it felt quite right.

Would I still be worthy if I had never been a mom?

What if I got tired and didn't work hard for a while, then would my worthiness be taken away?

Or what if I wasn't strong and was weak?

Friends, this is what I call a "thought spiral" and I've drowned in them more than once.

Maybe, I thought, this isn't question I *can* answer.

So I settled onto my knees the same way I had since Sunday school, right next to the little desk in the Residence Inn, and I spoke to God. He and I had been going through a rough spell since the kids left, and I'm woman enough to admit I was giving him the cold shoulder. My ideas on who God was were also shifting. I fought these feelings for a long time, trying to shove my beliefs about God into the same box that society had fit me inside of. For a while, space between the two of us felt like the answer, so that my relationship with whoever God was didn't become completely destroyed. This space grew a new respect for the Divinity that gently guided me, even when I didn't seek it out.

As I prayed, my heart felt like it was expanding from my chest and with every breath, an internal widening of love spread to the places where pain just was. I felt a profound sense of love from my Creator, this promise of purpose in my life. The purpose and the worthiness had nothing to do with the actions I was taking in that moment; it didn't have to do with me winning an award, or giving birth, or making money. The love that was being poured into me was coming just because of who I was. Because I was divinely created, with nothing to prove, and everything to gain, just being me was enough.

My entire body and mind were in peace, and what I wrote next came so clearly and powerfully that it just flowed onto my paper:

I am worthy, because I AM.

Because I exist. Because I breathe air and have a beating heart. Because there is a love bigger than all of us that sustains me and wants joy, love, and peace for my life. Because in all of existence, the past, the present, and the future, a moment was created in which I came to earth at a specific time with a specific purpose. I am worthy, because I Am. It felt so simple, yet so complicated. My answer had been there all along and was just waiting for me to stop covering it up with other things that had nothing to do with my actual worth. I breathed a sigh of relief and kept repeating the words, "*I am worthy because I am.*"

Accepting our essential goodness and acknowledging our incredible worth is not always easy. Accepting that there are some questions we aren't equipped to answer is not easy. Maybe instead of sacrificing the joy, we're meant to surrender to the peace?

I am worthy because I AM. And so are you.

I still deal with feelings of unworthiness. I still need to be reminded of all the little and big mysterious reasons why I deserve to be here and live fully. But writing it down, and uncovering the truth about who I am, allowing myself to surrender to peace and joy the same way I surrender to faith, has given me a bit of an anchor.

Maybe this is a place you need to pause. Do you believe that you are worthy? Think about it, and take your time. Do you believe that you have intrinsic worth that no one, and no circumstance, can take away? That you are exactly who you need to be, born at the time you were meant to be here? If you are struggling with this, this could be a great affirmation to place on your mirror or set in your phone to remind yourself. You are exactly who you need to be, you are exactly where you need to be, and you matter because you are YOU.

Staying anchored, though, is a little more complex. Fostering an internal sense of love and belonging on a daily basis is a heck of challenge. I have to work at it, and you may have to work at it too. After that day at the hotel, though, I knew exploring that big question was something I wanted to integrate into my routine.

I use three tools to remind myself that I belong in this life exactly as I am. You can use these tools, too:

1 **Talk to yourself.** (Probably not on the subway or in an Uber, though.) As women, we know where our army of family, kids, friends, and coworkers need to be at all times in the day, and we know what they need from us. We know our loved ones' best traits and what makes them tick and flourish, but we often don't know ourselves the same way. We look in the mirror to brush our hair or our teeth every day, but we don't really *look* at who is staring back at us.

To help remind myself who I am, I look in the mirror every morning and converse with myself. I look at that girl with the morning hair and the spinach in her teeth and I pay her a compliment: "I am _____ ". Some days, I am silly. Some days, I am strong. Plenty of hard days when I can't come up with something that feels real, I just look into those sleepy eyes and declare "I AM." Throughout the day, if I feel myself creeping toward self-doubt, I remind myself of whatever it was I said that morning.

2   **Talk to God/Universe/the Divine.** Your religious beliefs are of no consequence to me, but your spirituality is. Spirituality is how you take care of your soul, how you renew it and uncover truth and find power to sustain yourself even when things get hard. Spirituality is strengthened through connection to a Higher Power. Whatever you believe that Higher Power to be, you have access to it. You don't have to do this all alone. Prayer, meditation, and quiet moments of reflection are all ways to quiet the noise and let your soul receive answers that don't have anyone else's agenda attached to them. Talking to God and inviting the Universe to guide me has revealed so much clarity and knowledge about my path and who I am that I would not be able to receive any other way. If you don't know where to start, that's okay! Sit for five minutes in the morning, and ask the question, "God, Universe, or whatever I believe in, what would you like me to know today?" And then start writing.

3 **Talk to your people.** It's hard to feel worthy and valued if the people around you drag you down. I used to try really hard to fit in to groups of friends. If I wasn't invited to a party or a vacation, it would break my heart and I would wonder what was wrong with me. Once a friend told me something that changed the way I view my relationships. She said, "Others have permission to feel however they do about me."

Once I gave people permission to have their own opinion about me, I stopped trying to control it and obsessing over whether or not I was accepted. I stopped putting time into relationships that were one sided, and instead, I have a very small tribe full of supportive and encouraging people who help me thrive and reel me back in if they see me going off course. My main tribe starts with my family, and we have a few close friends whom we share our lives with. Letting go of relationships that weren't serving me was very hard at first. But now my energy isn't being attacked by people who don't have my best interest in mind, and I am surrounded by people who regularly remind me that I am worthy.

Know that you are deeply valuable and very much chosen for the incredible life you're getting ready to lead. You were given gifts, use them. You were given challenges, rise to them. You were given doubts, search that beautiful soul. If you weren't worthy of this glorious life, you simply wouldn't have been chosen to live it. Because of the light and love that is inherently within you, because of a greater love that encircles you, you are worthy, you are perfect, you are whole. Embrace who and what you are, and if you need to, stay anchored to these words: *I am worthy because I AM.*

When I sat down with my Clarity Map to answer the question "Why am I worthy?" I started listing the reasons why, karmically, I deserved success: I'd experienced failure, I'd experienced pain, I'd given to others. Then I moved on to hard facts: I was about the age where I should hit it big, I had a degree, I'd volunteered, I went to church even when I didn't want to. I wadded up the list and threw it away. Finally, I wrote something true. Not about my accolades or accomplishments, but about my attributes:

I am worthy because I do my best. I show up even when it's hard, and if I get something wrong the first hundred times, I try again.

The reasons you're worthy don't have anything to do with balancing the scales or punching the time card. It isn't a quantitative thing; it's about the essential incalculable stuff that makes you who you are. So, sister, it's time for you to answer the question "Why am I worthy?" Tell me why it's time for you to show up for yourself, and write it next to this question on your map, in your journal, or in this book (refer back to page 82).

We've set our intentions. We've discovered our intrinsic worth. And now we need to learn to set down the things we've been carrying with us for too long that don't actually serve us.

9

WHO CAN I
Serve?

Mike and I met Randy at church the week after we moved to Nashville. The first time we spoke, he introduced himself as "Randy, the guy who used to cook meth in his kitchen," and all I could say back was "Hi! I'm Ashley. I don't cook anything in my kitchen." I'd never met anybody like him; his wide, toothless smile sparkled more than any well-veneered celebrity's, and he was disarmingly open and honest about his past.

Every Sunday, as the weeks wore on and the crackling brown leaves of winter gave way to the first soft touches of green, Randy would find us in church, and we'd talk about work and life and family. I asked him what he did, and he told me he was the manager for the same halfway house that helped him get back on his feet. He also mentioned that he helped out at a nonprofit lifting heavy loads of furniture, clothing, and toys that went to families in need in rural Tennessee. He stretched his sixtysomething-year-old back and winced.

"Wow. That's incredible," I mumbled, feeling a little awestruck and maybe a little humbled. I'm not going to pretend I hadn't made assumptions about who he was.

Randy's life was not easy. Some of the stories he told me from "way back" were harrowing. It seemed like nothing less than a miracle that he had made it out alive. He didn't have much, not time or money, but what he did have he gave to serving others. Even me.

Mother's Day rolled around, and I had decided I didn't want to celebrate Mother's Day anymore. We'd call our own mothers, of course, but I couldn't stand the thought of an austere bouquet of flowers standing in for the breakfast in bed and homemade cards I was used to receiving from my kids. I shut myself inside, until the phone rang. It was Randy.

"Hey, Ashley, do you have plans tonight?"

I searched wildly through my mind for an excuse, but I couldn't lie to Randy.

"No, I don't." I mumbled.

"Great!" he exclaimed, his thick southern drawl growing energetic. "Can I take you (and Mike) to dinner for Mother's Day? To the best Mexican restaurant ever?"

I could hardly wrap my head around the kindness, sincerity, and love in his offer. I lowered my head and listened as he went on about the three kinds of salsas and the carnitas tacos and the Mexican coke in real glass bottles. I was within a millimeter of weeping uncontrollably.

He knew I didn't have kids with me to celebrate; I had told him our story, and he had shared with me his. He knew that I would be hurting today. He wanted to be sure I felt seen. I was a mother, even though my children were gone, and I can't tell you how meaningful it was to have somebody acknowledge that.

"I would absolutely love that, Randy. Thank you."

A few hours later he was in our driveway, long, gray beard freshly clipped and that grin of his shining as brilliantly as ever.

I used to think that to change the world, or really make an impact, I needed to do something *big*. That to make a difference I must reach a large amount of people, and that if I couldn't figure out how to do that, then the time I was spending serving wasn't that important. I'd overlook the human being who was right in front of me, spinning my wheels on how to reach ten other people. But Randy taught me what it means to serve. It means that we see people, right as they are, for who they are, and we love them. It means we pour all that we have into lifting them up, and we do it without any expectation of getting anything in return. Service means bringing love to a soul who needs a shot of courage. It means sitting with a friend who's in the middle of pain sometimes, and other times it means cutting the grass for a neighbor. I have found that the most life-changing acts of service are done one person at a time. As we are able to connect and reach out to each other, one connection at a time, real impact and meaningful relationships are created.

Randy was right, they were the best tacos ever. In fact, it was one of the most incredible nights of my life. Randy held space for me to talk about the kids when I wanted to. He listened intently and compassionately, taking a break from his beloved carnitas to take in every word. He was vulnerable; he told Mike and me about how his mom died traumatically, and how hard it was for him to walk through the holiday without her. He smiled and said that celebrating me would help both of us.

For hours, we talked, about everything from friendship to heavy metal bands (I didn't try to convert him into becoming a Belieber, but don't think I wasn't tempted). When the check came, Mike pulled out his wallet but Randy protested. He said he was excited to pay for our dinner, and that he had switched his budget around for the month to make room for this. Not only had Randy seen me and held space for me, but he had sacrificed, just to show me that I was loved and important. Later, he told me that he shows up for people the way he wished people would have shown up for him. That statement has become a bit of a North Star for me.

The very next morning, the third question popped into my head during meditation: *Who can I serve today?* It was simple. If Randy, a man who had experienced what many would characterize as immense suffering, had it in him to lift others up, then so did I. Asking that small, simple question every day, inspired by Randy, has brought incredible meaning to my life, mindfulness to my actions, and (I hope) some level of good to the world that I live in.

If you have love in your heart, *you* have a gift to give. As long you're willing to share that love, you can make an impact. It isn't always easy to know where to begin, and the idea of integrating service into daily life can be overwhelming, but I promise, it isn't as complex or consuming as it seems. Here are three simple ways you can begin to serve those around you:

1 **See someone.** When I answer the question *Who can I serve today?*, it allows me to see people on a more personal level. You might notice that your coworker is juggling a lot of things, or your sister needs a day off from wrangling the kids, or the cashier at the grocery store simply needs to be told what a great job she is doing moving things along quickly. Seeing someone means that we notice the way they are showing up for their life and the world around them, and we acknowledge their efforts. It means that we really listen to what they are telling us, and if we have a hunch they are tired and worn out, then we step in to give them some reprieve. When we see people as they are, we get this magical opportunity to look outside of ourselves and celebrate the courage that is taking place around us.

2 Hold space for someone. I first recognized the power behind holding space for someone during a podcast interview hosted by an author and a therapist. It was one of the most raw interviews I had ever been a part of, and my answers were both heavy and life-giving for me. When I was finished sharing my story of grief and triumph, we all just sat there in silence. The therapist said, "We could go on with this interview, but I feel like we need to just sit in this place and hold space for everything that you've been through. Moving on to the next questions right now feels too rushed, and I want to honor everything you've just shared with us."

We were all crying, *together.* It was one of the few interviews that I didn't feel used for my story, something I quickly learned when media outlets wanted to share my story for higher rankings or so that their list could grow. After a while, I became aware that I wasn't being asked to share my life on others' platforms to help reach women who were brokenhearted and needed guidance, I was being used so that they could benefit from my trauma. This therapist honored my story by holding space for me, lifting me up, and supporting me. Holding space for someone means that you do so with zero expectations in return. It can look as simple as sending a gift to a grieving woman, fully knowing that you do not need a thank-you note back.

After that experience, I better understood how to hold space for someone. It means that we honor what they've been through. It can be powerful to sit and listen, or sit with a friend who needs support and just have them know that you are right there as they go through it. Holding space for someone doesn't mean that we come up with solutions to fix their problems, it means we are supportive and emotionally available as they go *through* them. I now have a calendar where I write in important anniversary dates for people I know. It helps me remember to reach out on important dates that can be triggering, such as the year mark of the loss of a loved one, and it creates space for me to be supportive.

3 Sacrifice for someone. I recently went to the house of a friend who just had a stillborn baby. I was traveling for work and happened to be in her city when everything happened. Mike was with me, but had meetings all day, so I took dinner to her family alone. Sitting together, I said, "I'm so sorry. I wish we were here longer and could do more." Her husband was still in shock, and he replied, "It's okay, this isn't convenient for anyone." I was struck by the wisdom of that response, even as he sat deeply grieving.

Grief, loss, heartache, stress, letdowns—none of it is convenient, which means we're called to show up for our people when it's not convenient for us, either. Putting our needs aside to show up for people is a pure gesture of love that puts someone's needs above our own. Real service is love in action, and love isn't selfish. It's sacrificial.

After you've identified your intention, and why you are worthy for it, it's time to explore who it will benefit. For me, because of my stated intention and my life experience, I knew that I would be serving women who felt like they were stuck in life. Easy. It isn't so easy for everyone to identify though.

One of my favorite clients, a teacher who was battling cancer *and* navigating the foster care system, had lived her life serving others. She was drained. Her intention was, "I make time for myself every single day," but she struggled to determine who it would serve. Then, something sparked inside of her, and a big smile crossed her lips. "I serve myself" she said softly.

The answer to "Who can I serve?" can be a group of people, an individual, and yes, even yourself. It's impossible to serve others when our well is dry. The real beauty, though, is that as you begin to live out your intention daily, you'll probably see it benefit all kinds of people.

Think for a moment about the types of people you could serve. Who are you regularly working with or surrounded by? What topic or issue raises your passion? Is there an underserved community that you see an opportunity to help? Then, referring back to page 82, write who you will serve through your intention next to that line.

Serving others has empowered me by making me look outside of myself and connect in real, human ways with those around me. Whether I personally know them, or am passing a stranger, I believe that people can be put in our paths for a purpose, but it's up to us to create what that purpose is.

It can be as simple as writing a note on your restaurant receipt to your waitress, or more thought out like showing up with dinner on a friend's doorstep. Service is love in action. The return that I receive when I put my love into action is even more love.

Our Clarity Map is really coming together now, and I hope you can see and appreciate all the progress you are making! Take a moment to acknowledge the effort you have put into yourself so far; I am so proud of you. Next, we're going to work on the obstacles that often get in the way of putting these positive intentions in place and set them down so we can move forward.

10

WHAT CAN I
Set Down?

During a sixteen-city speaking tour, at the beginning of each event, I asked the women to complete an exercise. There was a jar at the front of the room and next to it, another jar of small candles and a little sign that said, "Put your worry in the vase and take a light in its place."

I didn't know if anyone would participate, whether they thought we were going to raffle off a boat or put them on a giant email list. But without fail, at every stop, the jar would fill up with hundreds of worries. Many women believed they were stuck, many believed they were alone. Some believed that they needed to be better parents or wives or business owners. The one thing that all the worries had in common was that they carried weight. Too much weight.

To close out the night, I directed the women to take out another person's worry from the jar, walk through a light labyrinth, and set it down at the end. The light labyrinth was outlined by small, white paper bags, each with a candle inside. We turned off the lights in the room, and the candles created a path that led to an opening where all the worries would be placed. It had become a path of power and hope, as women carried other women's worries for them; some even ripped them up before they set them down, creating a sense of connection among strangers. We don't have to carry our hard stuff alone.

I hadn't done the labyrinth yet, so on the last night of the tour, I decided to walk through it alone before the event. I walked to the dark room, lit by candles, to set down the worry and pain I had been carrying for a long time. I wrote my children's names on a small piece of paper and walked the labyrinth, repeating "I love you" the whole way through. At the end, I kissed my slip of paper and gently set it down.

The next morning, I got on a plane and wrote the next question in my journal:

What can I set down?

I've written down and meditated on it every day since. It reminds me that I don't have to carry anything into my day that doesn't serve me. It reminds me that I can re-open an old chapter without reopening an old wound. It reminds me that my story isn't over. Neither is yours. We all have something we carry into our day that we can set down: trauma, heartache, painful childhood memories, anger, shame. We just need to learn how to identify what it is that feels so heavy.

To guide my process of answering the question, I do a simple body scan each morning. I check in with my physical self to notice if I feel like I'm holding any anxiety, fear, anger, or stress anywhere. If my stomach feels tight, I might be holding on to anxiety about something. If my head feels dizzy or confused, oftentimes it means I've started comparing myself to others and have stopped listening to my gut. Once I identify the physical sensation, I ask myself, *What experience am I holding on to that is creating this feeling?* Sometimes the answer comes right away, and other times I have to think about it longer. The details can be tricky, and steps we've taken years ago (particularly painful ones) are not always easy to retrace. I've also done this work alongside a professional, and for you, it may be best to complete this work with a professional by your side. That's nothing to be ashamed of; you don't deserve to live with trauma forever, and if someone can help you move past that, it's well worth the effort.

Once I identify what I'm holding on to, I write it down. And then I put it into my very own worry jar, just like the one I had on tour. I call it my God Box. Yes, I have a God Box! When I'm worried or anxious about something, I write it down and put it into the box. It allows me to stop holding on to the worries in my body and in my mind, and to send them out to the bigger universe, or love, or God, or whatever it is that you believe in, to take care of it. This doesn't mean that I ignore issues that need to be resolved, it means that in that moment, when I have no control over changing a worry, I set it free so it doesn't have the power to keep weighing me down. Being able to trust that I am not the only one in charge in my life allows me to recognize that there's a bigger power that will help lay my worries to rest. My God Box holds everything from worrying about if I turned off my curling iron or not and I'm going to burn the entire house down (after I'd already checked three times), to trying to control the outcome of securing a work partnership that I've given my best efforts to. Not everything is taken care of in the exact way I hope it would be; that's not the point of the God Box. But it frees up the energy and space in my body so that I can focus on other things, and not keep holding on to problems that I can't immediately solve in the moment.

Some days you might have to set down the same thing over, and over, and over again. And that is okay. The physical act of writing it down allows you to release it from yourself, if even for a minute. The freedom of energy and weightlessness it will bring will allow space to open up for the types of things you WANT to be filled up with.

What have you been holding on to? Is there a fear that plays on repeat every time you think of a person or situation? Is there a relationship that has been hurting you and holding you back? Visualize yourself setting "it" down, watch yourself walking through your own labyrinth holding your own piece of paper. Notice the lights, feel the peace on the path. When you get to the end, kiss the paper that holds whatever it is that you need to set down, and gently place it on the floor. Or crumble it, or tear it to shreds, whatever it is that you need. Hold peace ever so gently in your hands.

The purpose of this exercise is to move forward, and forward motion becomes easier when we're able to let go of what's holding us back. In the last section, you did a really good job with letting go, and now, we are learning how to set something down. You might be wondering what the difference is between the two, and that's a really good question. Not letting go binds us to our past, which is why we spent time learning how to embrace our life so that it can serve us in our present. But not setting a worry down overwhelms our present with current anxieties. Our head can become so cluttered with the current realities of paying the bills, getting a mean text, hating our job, or counting calories that there becomes no room to take a proactive approach to our life because we are stuck reacting to everything that is stressing us out. Setting down current concerns that you have no control over in the present moment allows you to live your life from a place of building what you want, instead of reacting to what it is that you don't. You've just created a really powerful place to rest in your road map to clarity.

Take out your Clarity Map. What's holding *you* back? It could be an emotion or an unhealthy relationship or a past trauma. When I did Clarity Mapping for myself the first time, my intention terrified me. If you'll remember, I wrote down "I guide women to help uncover their power." What if I wasn't any good at guiding women? What if I failed? What if nobody connected with me? Fear kept me from beginning to write the course material, it kept me from sharing the practice, it kept me from sleeping more than two hours in a row at night. Without letting the fear go, I couldn't move forward.

So I wrote it down. I put it in my box. I set the worry down, not just one time, but enough times that it didn't keep me from taking the next step toward my goal.

Sometimes the pain still just feels like too much, and I believe that we all carry more on our shoulders than we need to and that setting down what doesn't serve us can be key in moving forward confidently (and comfortably!). It may seem easier just to soldier on, it might feel safer to take everything with us, than to examine what it is we really need. The problem is, we were never meant to carry it all, all the time. Yes, I know you can because you're strong and persistent, but you don't have to. You can set it down. And setting it down right now is exactly what I want to help you to do.

When I'm bringing extra emotional baggage into my day, I take five minutes to sit down and unpack it. Sometimes I do it during my morning routine and meditation, other times it's when I'm exhausted and screaming in my car. I prefer to deal with it *before* it gets to that point, but we're all doing our best! To start my unpacking, I ask myself how an emotion or experience ended up on my heart and what purpose it can serve on my journey. I set down the things that burden me and secure the things that bolster me. More often than not, after I've gone even just a little bit deeper, pain looks more like love, grief looks more like gratitude, envy looks more like admiration.

Now it's time for you to write your own "Unpacking List." I want to you to think about what you're carrying with you right now and why. Some of it you will set down for today, and other parts you will hold close to your heart. Whatever is on your heart, I want you to consider the value it holds instead of the heaviness it creates. Answer the following questions in a separate notebook or journal:

What are you taking with you?

Why are you taking it?

How can it serve you?

What do you need to set down?

Any time those shoulders grow weary, any time those feet start to ache, any time your heart feels heavy, you can sit down and take inventory. Moving forward slowly, intentionally, and mindfully is the perfect place to begin!

To identify the thing, or things, that are holding you

back, it might help to do a body scan like I mentioned earlier, to figure out where in your body feels tense. Sit in a quiet place and slowly move from head to toe, stopping to notice if you feel any sensations along the way. Write it down on the paper, savor every stroke of your pen, visualize that heavy weight lifting from your body as you set it down. How do you feel now? This exercise is great to do whenever you feel like you don't know how to keep moving forward. It can be done before large life decisions, or even just to get clear about how you want to intentionally live out your days. The most powerful part about this practice is that it is now a part of your toolkit, to pull out whenever your inner voice tells you that you need it.

Once you know what the thing, or things, are that you need to set down, write them down next to that question (refer to page 82).

We have one final question left in our Clarity Map, and it's all about figuring out and living out the truest version of yourself. Because we can do all the things we've talked about up until this point in the book, but if we still aren't allowing ourselves to be who we are, we aren't accepting the freedom that is waiting for us.

11

WHO IS THE TRUEST VERSION
of Myself?

Moving forward in my new world was dizzying. I had spent a long time unhappy, unfulfilled, and totally uncertain of who I was. I asked my morning questions and searched my soul, but as with any relationship, getting to know myself again took time, energy, and openness. So much had happened over the course of just a couple of years. None of it was expected. Even when the dust settled, it never seemed to land where I thought it would. My world was strange and unfamiliar; I felt like a stranger. I doubted every instinct and felt terrified by the sound of the wind, of my dog's feet on the floor, of my phone ringing to life. I had no identity, no sense of belonging in my body or spirit. I had no way home. Grief brings a feeling of intense homesickness, and a reality that you can never go back to the place you are longing for.

Mike longed for me as much as I longed for myself. He needed me as he waded, mostly alone, in our new world. He held my clammy hand in his and said, maybe it was even a plea, born of concern for me and desperation for us, "I just want my wife back. I just want to hold you and know that you're still here with me."

It broke my heart, for both of us. Overnight, he had lost his children and his wife. I didn't want to be lost anymore. The next morning, I got to work. I needed to come back to him, but first, I needed to come back to myself.

Who is the best version of myself? I wrote the words hurriedly on a rumpled journal page, in a rush only to get them out of me and feel proactive. I had nothing. The page stared back at me expectantly, like I was letting it down too.

I knew that I was a wife; a mother, with or without my children by my side; and an entrepreneur. I knew the actions I took every day to fulfill those roles, but underneath all these tasks and titles, everything else was a little hazy. I had been conditioned to "be good." Which meant that I was in a constant battle between feeling peace and trusting my intuition and doing things that I *thought* I was supposed to do, to appease everyone else. Often, doing what I thought was the "good" thing contradicted with what I felt, deep inside, was good for *me*. I didn't want to strive for the "best" me anymore, but the truest.

I scratched out the little scrawl and tried again.

Who is the truest version of myself?

I wanted to learn who I was, without titles, or expectations, or my fear of letting the people around me down, or having them get upset with me. To figure it out, I knew that I needed to strip everything away, start listening to myself, and not look to others for instructions on how to act or feel or think.

I looked at the page again.

Who is the truest version of myself?

I didn't have an answer yet, but it was okay. Grief was an opportunity to begin again, to let the habits and layers of fear fall away. I resolved to let my truth reveal herself. She came quicker than I thought she would, in a painful situation at work that ultimately revealed who I was at my core.

During a few of the months that I had spent fighting for our children in court, I'd left a dear friend and trusted employee in charge of helping run the entire operation, someone who told me not to worry and I didn't. This person had traveled and spent holidays with us. We had cried and prayed together. But once I returned, it was clear that something was wrong.

Our financial statements didn't make sense. Money was missing. There were a series of bizarre, enormous charges billed to us and contracts bearing my signature that I had never even seen before. I almost threw up when I looked at our account balance. There was hardly anything there. We weren't going to make payroll and rent, which were both due that week. And as I looked into it further, I realized the person I'd left in charge had led the company into this terrible situation. I couldn't believe it. I had been blindsided by someone I believed in with all my heart. At least, someone I thought I *should* believe in, even when the little twinges in my gut told me otherwise.

There had been warning signs before, but I ignored them. There were months where statements weren't turned in to me, days where I'd be charged for time worked when I knew it hadn't been, incidentals and expenses billed that I had never agreed to pay. It was all so muddy and convoluted, and I loved this person so much, that I suggested to myself the problem was *me*. This person was smarter than I was, I thought, more experienced, I had probably just misunderstood. I convinced myself that it wasn't worth rocking the boat, everyone else loved them just as much as I did, and a *good* CEO, and a *good* woman, wouldn't cause a fuss. I remember telling myself months before, *Ashley, be on your best behavior, let it go. People don't like it when you make a fuss.* I excused bad behavior and allowed myself to be taken advantage of. It was easier to sit back and let it happen than to stand up. I was trying to do the good thing, but sometimes the good thing isn't the right thing. Sometimes, it isn't the truest.

An hour later, I called my most-valued employee into my office and I fired them on the spot. They were furious. Their words made me feel small and broken. Their eyes practically glowed when they told me I "wasn't in a good place." They were right about that, I wasn't, but at least after months of fear and avoidance, I was present there. And I was at peace. I knew this was the right thing to do, for the health of my company, and ultimately, for myself.

Later that night, my husband got a phone call from the person I had fired. I could hear their voice, practically laced with gunpowder, through the receiver across the room. They told Mike that he needed to intervene in my company.

I was too emotional from losing the kids.

I was unable to think clearly and was going to be the cause of the collapse of my company if somebody didn't step in to save the day.

I wasn't a "good" leader.

For a moment, I panicked.

Could they be right?

Did I make a bad decision?

Am I too broken to lead this company?

I was embarrassed until I heard Mike's reply. It was what I had always needed to hear, not just from someone else, but from myself. He took a calm breath and said, "Ashley is the best CEO I know. Whatever decision she has made, I back her 100 percent. The last thing Ashley needs is to be 'saved' by anyone else. She knows who she is and I love her for it."

He was right.

The next few months were messy, chaotic, and uncomfortable, but change isn't a tidying up, it's renovating. For a while, I wanted nothing to do with my job. There were horrid rumors circulating about me, and our clients were nervous and wary to renew contracts since things had gotten so out of hand in my absence. Remember the anger we talked about earlier? I felt it. Daily. Hot and heavy, deep and justified. In many ways, I had to start all over again, but also, I had the opportunity to take some of my very first right steps.

I had hard conversations. I made people angry. I learned to accept that their anger was not my responsibility. I used my voice, knowing that the few who were listening were more important than the many who couldn't be bothered to hear. I hired people I felt good about, who believed in the company and wanted to make a difference. It was liberating. Finally, I stopped caring about being "good" and started caring about being ME. The pursuit of "goodness" had led me away from what was right and true. I think a lot of us know what it is to lose ourselves in that struggle.

From a very young age, many of us learn the language of who we are from those around us. Maybe we're defined by others as "pretty," "clever," or "sweet." Maybe we're "stupid" or "boring." Whatever the words may be, we hear them; many of us might even believe them. I was "good." It was the definition given to me by teachers and parents and coaches. It felt safe and needed. But it wasn't true because it never originated inside of me.

After things at the company began to calm down, I spent a few moments each morning reminding myself who I was and what was important to me. I looked at myself preshower in the mirror. I got comfortable with all the uncomfortable parts of that bare-naked starkness. I let that image in the mirror be the truest reflection of myself I would accept that day, no matter what anybody else said, no matter how anybody else reacted. In the silvery glass, I saw a healthy body that could move, I saw lines I had earned, lessons I had learned through love, laughter, and loss. I saw my parents, my dad's eyes and my mom's smile. I saw someone with promise. What came to mind wasn't the girl who wrote the book or started the business or married the awesome guy; it was the woman I saw in the bathroom mirror, who walked into her day knowing she was enough.

I looked at my reflection and asked her what she needed to hear. Three affirmations came to mind: *you have enough, you're doing enough, you are enough.*

I had an incredible determination and endurance to

get through hard crap. I had an ability to not give up that drove me forward, even when life was hard.

I was doing things that brought me joy. Some days I felt more capable than others, but each day I showed up committed to putting my heart into the world, and living with love and integrity.

I was becoming exactly who I was created to be. Everything I was searching for externally was all ready to be found inside of me. I was learning that I had everything I needed to find joy, love, and happiness, and I could stop worrying that I was falling short or disappointing other people.

Eventually, with patience and practice, I began to trust in the beautiful words on my own heart more than any words on someone else's lips. Eventually, what I saw was so much more than "enough"; it was abundance.

If it feels right to you, say something true to yourself. Head straight to the mirror; it's the best place to start taking a long, intentional look at the girl who is staring back at you. Notice who you are, acknowledge yourself and the way you show up. Tell yourself that you're doing a great job and start acknowledging the truth about who you are.

Who are you? Who are you *really*? Let's talk about it! These three questions help me uncover myself when being true to who I am is different than who other people are telling me I should be.

1 **What's underneath?** Beneath the job title, the social status, the clothes on your body, and the outside influences is you. If you can't remember who that is, it's time for a reunion. It's time to come back home to yourself. Who is the truest version of yourself? Don't overthink it; say out loud the first five things that come into your head. And that, sister, is where you will start. You don't need to worry about being good anymore, you just need to focus on being true.

2 **Why am I afraid?** This question involves some deep, honest introspection. I split my fear into two parts. First, I examine why I am afraid about not meeting other people's expectations about who I am. I write down all my feelings, because speaking them to life brings to light the dark places I try to keep buried. Fear doesn't need to be buried, it needs to be acknowledged.

I usually notice that my fears about *other people*'s thoughts of me are what are actually keeping me from living my truest life. Which means that I care more about acceptance by other people than I do about living true to myself. Ouch.

Next, I ask myself, *Why does it feel scary to be true to me?* The answers to that question are powerful. Now I know where to start, what to work on, and how to keep moving forward.

3 **Who am I upsetting?** There are basically two answers to this. If you are living your truest life, you're going to upset other people. Not everyone has the same ideas, desires, hopes, and experiences. We're not supposed to. And what I have found is that it's usually those who aren't living *their* truest lives that we upset the most. It can feel overwhelming and triggering to see a woman powerfully own who she is and act from that space if you are a person who is insecure with your own role in life. Seeing someone live free and true threatens our understanding of our place in the world. So those whose journey has not led them to this place you're at will often be upset. It's hard, but we need to accept that truth. On the other hand, if you are not living your truest life, the main person you are upsetting is yourself. Understanding who you are giving more weight to can help you make changes that allow you to live true.

Let's turn to our Clarity Map. When are you the happiest in your skin and in your spirit? I want you to close your eyes and really see that woman. What is she doing? How does she feel on the inside? What is she wearing and saying and how is she acting? Does she have a morning routine she sticks to? Does she create quiet space for herself? Feel the power in her, the peace she carries, the clarity her mind feels, and the big love that's making her heart beat.

She isn't a daydream, she's a reality. You might not always see her, but she's inside you. Let's invite her to join us today.

On the piece of paper (refer to page 82), you can write a word that embodies her, you can draw a picture, you can even give her a name (I did). When describing her, I want you to feel as free as possible. Getting closer to her is a part of this journey too.

12

FINISHING THE
Clarity Map

et's take a moment to honor and celebrate the work you've started. In walking through each of these five questions—what is your intention, why are you worthy, who can you serve, what can you set down, who is the truest version of myself—what came up for you? What was raised to the surface that you've been keeping down? I hope that you feel a little bit clearer already, and ready to move, because we're about to take the first few steps beyond. In this chapter, you're going to take the work you started with each of the five questions and develop that into *your* Clarity Map. You are ready for this, you are deserving of this. Sister, you're not stuck anymore. Let's move forward together!

Let me start by showing you a finished version of my own map, so you can see where we're going. If it looks overwhelming, don't worry, I'll walk with you through

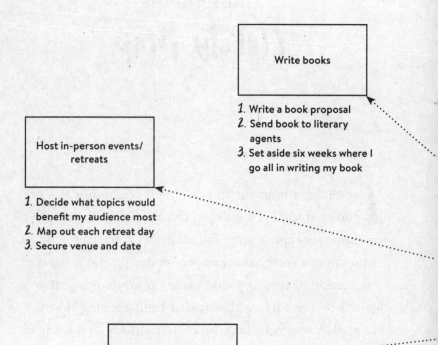

Write books

1. Write a book proposal
2. Send book to literary agents
3. Set aside six weeks where I go all in writing my book

Host in-person events/ retreats

1. Decide what topics would benefit my audience most
2. Map out each retreat day
3. Secure venue and date

Create accessible online workshops

1. Identify what my audience wants the most in help and community
2. Dedicate one week to filming and content creation
3. Set up a launch team

the steps, hand you every tool you need, and cheer you on as you walk into the beautiful life that's been waiting for you.

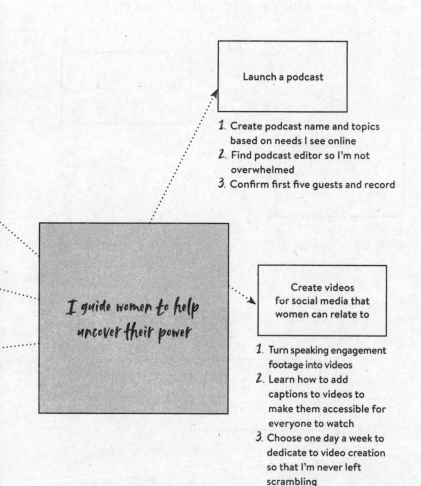

Launch a podcast

1. Create podcast name and topics based on needs I see online
2. Find podcast editor so I'm not overwhelmed
3. Confirm first five guests and record

I guide women to help uncover their power

Create videos for social media that women can relate to

1. Turn speaking engagement footage into videos
2. Learn how to add captions to videos to make them accessible for everyone to watch
3. Choose one day a week to dedicate to video creation so that I'm never left scrambling

Now, here is a blank version of the map. You can either write into the spaces below, or draw these boxes in your journal or on another piece of paper. Focus your attention on the middle of your map—that is where you'll write your intention, which we discussed in chapter 7. You'll see

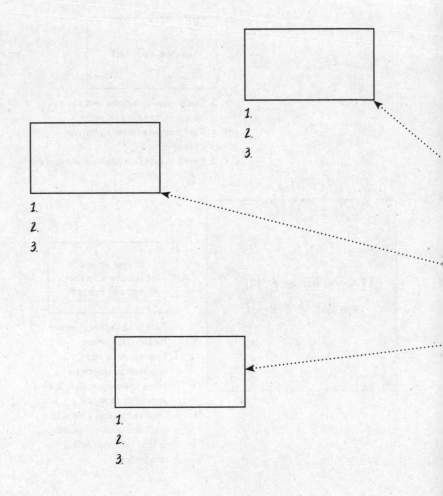

we've drawn five boxes surrounding your main intention.

In each box, write an action item that you can complete to bring your intention to life, a tangible step that you can take to turn an abstract goal into a real achievement. See my example on the next page.

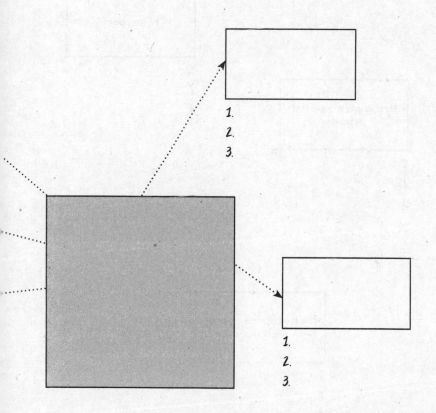

1.
2.
3.

1.
2.
3.

Write books

Host in-person events/retreats

Create accessible online workshops

Create videos for social media that women can relate to

Launch a podcast

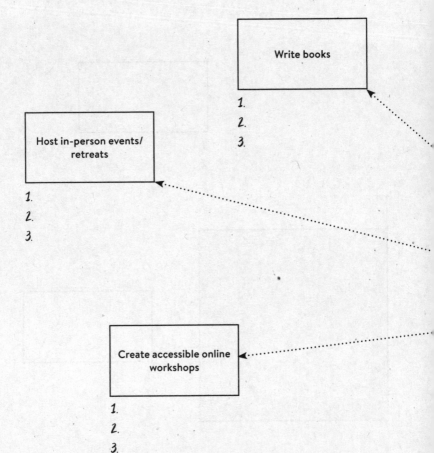

Write books

1.
2.
3.

Host in-person events/retreats

1.
2.
3.

Create accessible online workshops

1.
2.
3.

Each action item I chose was a way for me to reach out to the women I wanted to serve, a way for me to begin living out my intention.

The actions you select don't have to be grand gestures; they can be small, meaningful steps that make sense for you and your life. The goal is to create forward motion,

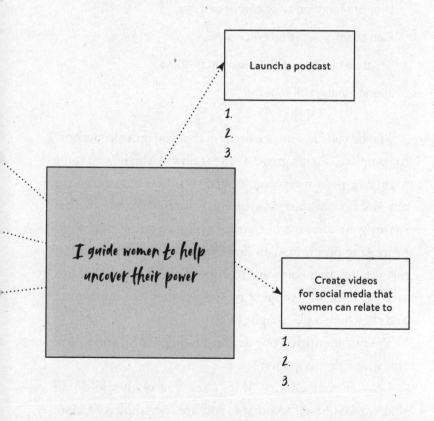

Launch a podcast

1.
2.
3.

I guide women to help uncover their power

Create videos for social media that women can relate to

1.
2.
3.

but we don't need to break any land speed records. Go at your own pace and keep in mind that the biggest joys can come from the littlest of things. If, like our rock star mama from earlier, we want to create more time with family, we could choose actions like:

Eat dinner together every other evening

Limit screen time to one hour per day

Plan a family vacation twice a year

Create a family gratitude journal to share

Spend Sundays all together

Maybe you have an action item that you don't know how to complete. That's great! Write it down! Maybe you want to host in-person retreats for your business but don't have any idea how to start. Maybe you want to write a book that shares your message but you're still navigating that word processing program. You don't need to know how to do it just yet, just that you want to know. Whether your dreams are big or small, complex or simple, they are important, and they have a place right here.

We just identified our actions and now it's time to act! But where do we go first?

Look at your Clarity Map. (Yes, you really did do all that work yourself. And yes, you are incredible.) We are going to write a "to-do list" for each of the five action items. I'll walk you through an example on my own map.

One action item that stood out to me was video content. Creating empowering video content for my online audience was something that I found gratifying, something that would make a tremendous impact on the people who consumed it, and something that was easy for me to do. Once I identified that as one of my starting places, I got into the nitty-gritty of how to make it happen. I created my to-do list. I brainstormed three tasks (you can choose as many as you like, but I always land around three to five) that I would need to take on to complete the overall action and I added them to my Clarity Map:

Turn speaking engagement footage into videos.

Learn how to add captions to videos so they are accessible for everyone to watch.

Choose one day a week to create video content so that I'm never left scrambling.

Now my Clarity Map looks like this:

Write books

1. Write a book proposal
2. Send book to literary agents
3. Set aside six weeks where I go all in writing my book

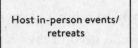

Host in-person events/ retreats

1. Decide what topics would benefit my audience most
2. Map out each retreat day
3. Secure venue and date

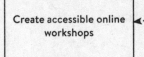

Create accessible online workshops

1. Identify what my audience wants most in help and community
2. Dedicate one week to filming and content creation
3. Set up a launch team

Take a minute to write down to-do lists under each of your action item boxes. As you write down what you need to do to bring that key action to life, remember that if you don't know all the answers, you can figure them out! It's totally okay to list skills that you need to learn to get there.

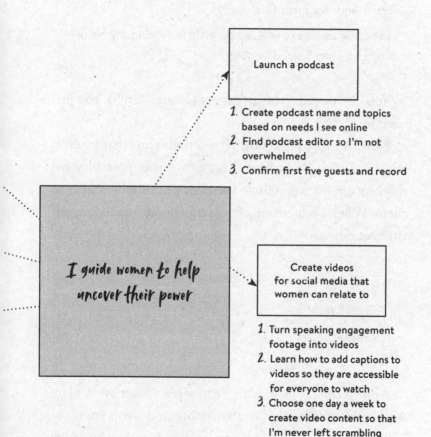

Launch a podcast

1. Create podcast name and topics based on needs I see online
2. Find podcast editor so I'm not overwhelmed
3. Confirm first five guests and record

I guide women to help uncover their power

Create videos for social media that women can relate to

1. Turn speaking engagement footage into videos
2. Learn how to add captions to videos so they are accessible for everyone to watch
3. Choose one day a week to create video content so that I'm never left scrambling

When I addressed "Write books," for example, my list looked like this:

Write a book proposal—need to research what this looks like.

Send it to literary agents, or pray that one finds me! Will ask friends for introductions.

Set aside six weeks where I go all in in writing my book—find out when I can schedule.

You don't need to be an expert (I sure wasn't); you just need be willing to learn.

Now let's focus in on the *three* action items that you feel will have the most impact and create the most forward momentum for you. Circle these, or put numbers next to them. When I selected my key action items, I asked myself three questions:

Is it motivating?

Is it meaningful?

Is it manageable?

And that's it, you're off to the races! You have a plan. You know exactly what you are going to do, you know exactly who you're doing it for, you know exactly why you're doing it, and you have actionable steps to take for three areas that you feel passionate about. Start moving through your to-do list and see how quickly you gain momentum toward your goals. If you get stuck on one item on the list, move on to another to keep that momentum going. YOU are ready. This is YOUR journey. Everything that you have been waiting for is right in front of you.

Ask yourself the five questions daily, which will help bring intention to your days. I reexamine this map about once a quarter. It helps me track how much progress I have made, and also I can evaluate what needs to change and where my time and attention should shift to based on what's going on in my life. Hang this map where you'll see it every day, and let's get to work!

PART THREE

Reclaim

YOUR

Power

Clarity Mapping has helped me reclaim my voice, my purpose, and my power in so many ways, and I truly believe it can for you, too. It took me a couple of years to uncover what living life looked like after everything I knew about it was shattered, but asking myself the five questions we explored in the last part and drawing a map that I could follow to get to where I wanted to go quite literally transformed me in the darkest moments of my life. I am excited that the work I did can now help you.

But it's important to note that just because you start taking some powerful steps doesn't mean it's easy to stand back up after you've been knocked down. Your legs feel wobbly, your head feels dizzy, and your heart feels as fragile as an eggshell. At least, that's how I felt. But I was up, I was moving forward, I knew what I wanted, and I was determined to get there.

I still had a lot of emotional triggers from our loss. No amount of clarity or mindfulness was going to remove those obstacles from my path, so I needed to learn how to navigate knowing that occasionally I was going to be face-to-face with something or someone that could hurt me. Reclaiming your power isn't about eliminating pain; it's understanding that though pain may be a part of your experience, it isn't a part of your identity. After Clarity Mapping became a part of my practice, I spent a long time wondering how I would sustain forward momentum when life got tough. The key for me when it came to maintenance was less about where I wanted to go, and more about who I wanted to be when I got there.

I wanted to be the Ashley who bravely played football with the boys at recess because she wasn't afraid. I wanted to be the Ashley who used her voice to speak up when things were wrong. I wanted to be the Ashley who believed in miracles and knew she could do really hard things, and who didn't care what anyone else thought. I wanted to be empowered, inspired, and connected, and I wanted to shout all of it from the rooftops. (I can be very shouty when I want to be.)

So, how do you reclaim and stay connected to your power? How do you keep moving forward when the path gets a little uneven? Theoretically, the answer is easy! You keep showing up, you commit to yourself every day, you get out of bed and scream "I AM HERE!" at the top of your lungs before the alarm even goes off. On a practical, personal level, it's all a little bit more complex: You take ownership of your thoughts and your actions. You make mistakes, and instead of letting them stop you, you give yourself grace and you learn. Above all else, you believe in yourself ferociously, and when you see yourself living out your carefully crafted intention, you darn well celebrate it. When I'm feeling unsteady, I remind myself how far I've come. I look around at my world, my gently cultivated territory, and remember that this journey has been deeper than going from one place to another. It's been my becoming. And I like the woman I've had to become to get here.

Through the work you've done in these pages reframing your thoughts and Clarity Mapping, you've discovered that many of the answers you seek are already inside you. I shared my path, but *you* have uncovered your own. Take a moment to let that victory sink in. I hope you're as proud of you as I am. The movement you have already made is miraculous, so let's keep going! Before we gallop off into the sunset, there are a couple things I want you to remember as you move forward:

1 **Living with clarity and power does not mean living perfectly, it means living mindfully.** Any recovering perfectionists out there? Hi! Here's the good news I have for you: none of us are going to get this completely right all the time. We're not supposed to. It's about noticing disruptive thoughts or actions and taking positive steps to change them.

2 **Maintaining forward momentum is hard work.** Remember what I said in the beginning? This isn't a shortcut. There's no magic wand that summons every-thing we've ever wanted out of life. But the work *is* magical because it's yours. And you get to see how strong you really are when you keep pressing forward. If you start feeling tired as your new life unfolds, congratulations! You are a human being like the rest of us! If it starts to get hard, it doesn't mean you're doing something wrong, it probably means you're doing something right.

Whenever you feel yourself slowing down, I want you to remember six affirmations that will help reignite your power, each of which we'll explore in the final pages of this book. I'm calling these the "I AM Affirmations," because they declare what is true about you, and you can claim them. They are:

I AM a Fighter
I AM Loud
I AM Not Alone
I AM Safe
I AM the Rainbow
I AM Free

You are on the top of your mountain, don't be afraid to shout it! The affirmations I've chosen are precious to me. I've whispered them and I've yelled them. I've written them on sticky notes and emailed them to myself. When I get down about everything I'm not, they remind me of everything I AM. Take them and remember that you ARE, too.

13

I AM A
Fighter

I am a fighter. Literally. Boxing has become a sacred part of my daily routine. I started because I thought it would help me release my anger, but what it did was help me reveal my power.

Mike was the one who stepped into the ring first. He went without me because I was too afraid to try something so completely out of my comfort zone. It seemed violent and loud. I pictured a bunch of sweat-slicked, bloody-faced Rocky Balboa types sipping on raw egg yolk shakes and jumping rope until their legs fell off. Not exactly my scene.

When he came home from his first class, an hour he described as "whaling on the heavy bag," he had a new spark in his eye.

"Ashley, you have got to come with me next time! I think this is exactly what we both need in our lives!" he panted, still red in the face and hot with adrenaline.

We had lost our consistent workout routine at the same time we lost our kids. We gave ourselves lots of grace (as one should), and for a long spell, we made a sport of watching Netflix on the couch and ordering Postmates. I longed to move my body and knew I needed an outlet. My temper was short and my nerves were fried. I was holding on to a lifetime of anger, and it was beginning to seep out when I least expected it.

"Really?" I asked him, clinging to the television remote as if it were some kind of talisman protecting me from the ills of this strange physical activity.

"Really," he assured me, wrapping me up in a big, sweaty hug. I decided I would give it just one shot.

The next day we went to the boxing gym together. The trainer taught me how to wrap my hands properly, spreading my fingers apart and starting with the wrap around my wrist, then lacing it up over my fingers, making sure each bone in my hand was covered and protected. I chose the pink hand wraps (naturally) and only half paid attention, assuming I would only be going through with it once. All I had to do was try, appease Mike, and make it back to the couch.

The trainer walked me over to the heavy bag, and I

stared up at the big faceless column hanging down from the ceiling on its chain, swinging just a little, back and forth, and . . . WHAM . . . I hit it, and I hit it hard. The feeling of transferring all the pent-up emotion I had been holding on to to an object outside of me gave me a rush of electricity that moved up my entire body so quickly that I couldn't help but punch again! With that first punch onto my bag, I knew I had just discovered an important outlet. I signed up for my own membership that day and bought my own gloves.

I had a session one morning just as a big, rumbling Tennessee storm was coming in. We had been training for about a year, and I had been growing mentally and physically stronger than I had been in a very long time. Our trainer, Jarrod, became more than a boxing instructor; he became one of our best friends. While my body was physically transforming through our workouts, my mind was transforming, too. He pushed Mike and me hard. He knew what we were capable of, and it was the first time that we felt like we had someone in this new city of ours that was *really* cheering for us. Jarrod helped us realize just how far we could go, and the days where I didn't think I could lift my arm one more time, he taught me that I could raise it a thousand more times if I had to. Each session was almost like going to therapy, and Mike and I shared a mutual relationship in helping each other overcome limiting mind-sets that were trickling into other areas of our lives. Boxing became the best form of individual and couples' therapy we could have possibly received.

That day, I felt off in the ring, a little tentative, distracted by the rain slapping against the roof. We were doing mitt work, which means that the trainer holds up pads and he yells out combinations that I have to quickly follow to hit them. It's not the kind of thing you want to mess up. If you do, you get clocked in the head. Dodging punches, coming within an inch of a punch to the face, is terrifying. I kept flinching and moving backward. I was clumsy and slow when a punch would come my way. I ducked and swayed and pivoted the best that I could but Jarrod knew something was up.

"Embrace the storm, Ashley! Lean into it so you don't lose your balance and you can make your next move!"

His words nearly knocked me to the mat.

Embrace the storm.

My mind was racing. Another swing from him came, and instinctively I flinched again. He threw his arms down.

"Dag gammit, Ashley!" Jarrod yelled (even though he looks tough, I've never heard him cuss). "I said embrace the storm! You already know I'm going to hit you. This isn't about trying not to get hit. You know it's coming and there's nothing you can do to stop it. Embrace the storm so you can embrace your power. When you take the hit, then you can use your power to come back with all your might. Don't let it stop you, don't lose the momentum."

I left the ring ten minutes later, exhausted, out of breath, but totally inspired. I carried his words with me, determined to keep moving forward.

Embrace the storm.

The punches were coming. It was inevitable, it was planned, but for the first time I really saw that I wasn't there to avoid them; I was there to fight. I wasn't there to learn how to conserve my power; I was there to learn how to free it. We put so much energy into avoiding the things that scare us that often we forget that we can choose to put that time and intention into overcoming them. What if life has nothing to do with ducking from pain and everything to do with learning how to confront it, head on?

What if, like a deep-rooted tree, we're built for the storms that we weather? What if we need these turbulent seasons in life to grow, to learn about who we are, and to uncover the power inside of us? If all this is true, then we need to stop trying to prevent chaos and let it show us that we can prevail. What if you are a deep-rooted tree? What if, like me, you're a fighter? A person with the will, courage, determination, ability, or disposition to fight, or struggle.

If we know our purpose, our worth, ourselves, if we walk into each day believing in our ability to move forward, the storm is nothing to be afraid of. Many of us are more resilient, more prepared, more determined than we think, but we'll never know it unless we step into the ring and embrace the storm. You've reframed your negative thoughts, you've reimagined your future and drawn the map. The journey isn't easy, so it's time to reclaim your power. I want to leave a mark of courage so deep inside of you that you are empowered to proclaim, "I AM A FIGHTER" at the top of your lungs and really *believe* it.

When I feel myself wanting to flinch in the midst of a struggle, I use three key strategies to recenter and stand strong. I call it the lean, learn, and defend mind-set. Lean into it, learn from it, defend that belief in yourself with everything you've got. Life is going to hit you, but if you continue to get back up, you continue to move forward. Here's what it looks like in action:

1 Lean into it. This is the hardest part. We decide to embrace the storm because we understand its inevitability and we accept it. We watch the clouds coming, we grab the steering wheel and trust ourselves to captain the ship.

My grandpa is a fisherman. He's spent thousands of hours chartering boats to take himself, family, and strangers salmon fishing on Lake Michigan. I had the special honor of going once when I was ten, but after the freezing winds and having to pee in a bottle, I vowed to never go again.

I asked him once what he does when the weather gets rough, and he introduced me to a concept where the ship is moving forward with enough power that it can steer right through the storm, instead of having the storm crash it every which way onto the waves. The captain of the ship has a very important job if this happens, and it's to keep the front of the ship pointing directly into the waves to steer through them safely.

The wind and the waves will try to roll you over sometimes. Push through with full, forward momentum. Use your power. Lean in.

2 **Learn from it.** For a long time, I thought that pain was meant to destroy me, to bring me down and make me question who I was and what life is. One morning, around the time of the anniversary date of when we became a family of four, I was getting ready to go to a lunch meeting. My body and my heart always react to these anniversaries, past emotions and feelings get stirred up, and it all feels incredibly mucky to wade through. I was sitting on the floor curling my hair, and I just lost it, wailing right there on the floor. My sobs got deeper and faster, and

I was gasping for air. I realized there was no way out of that moment, that I needed to feel it. I yelled out, "Pain! What do you want from me? What do you want to teach me right now? Why? Why? Why? I'm listening!" I got quiet, reached for my journal, and one word popped into my head: *love.*

The pain and anger I felt that day were real and visceral and consuming, but they weren't forever. What *was* forever was the love I had for my children. I listened to pain, and she taught me. I began to trust that these moments of pain were here to teach me. Some days, learning is hard.

3 **Defend it.** And by it, I mean yourself. Usually when the storm rages, the first thing to go is our belief in ourself. We don't believe we're brave or courageous enough to get through it; we stop trusting our intuition because how could it have steered us so wrong in the first place? We start believing that perhaps the pain is our own fault, we should have done more of this and less of that, we should have protected ourselves or our family better. We feel powerless in the very moments we need the most strength. Defend yourself; don't belittle that girl in the mirror when you should be empowering her.

When I started boxing, I thought I did it because it was a good outlet for my anger. After two years, though,

I finally realized why it was I was so smitten with the ring. It was during a session while I was just tearing apart the bag. I mean, I was hitting so fast and so hard I could hardly keep up with myself. There was nobody to show off for, no award to be won, and nothing to beat; it was just me and my bag. The harder I hit, the more energy I created. Usually after working out that long I would start to slow down and get tired, but not this time. Suddenly a loud thought rang between my ears, like someone was announcing for me to listen over the speakers, *I am not fighting anymore because I'm angry, I'm fighting because I'm freaking powerful.* Fighting from a place of power, instead of a place of anger, has created endurance, peace, and purpose in my life. I am a fighter. And, sister, you are too.

14

I AM
Loud

I vividly remember the day I lost my voice.

We were sitting in the courtroom, Mike was standing behind me (because nobody cared enough to make sure he had a chair), our attorney was to my left, and the opposing counsel to my right. We both sat facing the judge, who sat elevated on the stand just like on TV. The court reporter typed furiously at her little table, occasionally reminding the judge of a motion he needed to rule on. The monotonous sound of the keys clacking away was the one noise that for some reason rang out loud in my brain. It was like the telltale heart, with a legal twist.

The kids' social worker and court-appointed guardian were behind us along with a handful of other people in this room whose voices and faces were nothing but a murmuring blur. Our attorney had just argued passionately on our behalf, and a motion to remove the kids from our home had been denied. It was a victory. We were safe, together, for a while longer. I could breathe, until the next motion was filed, the next court date set.

Before we were dismissed, the opposing side was allowed to speak once more. At first, it was a few unkind words. Then, false accusations. Then, complete character assassination. I remember hearing what they said and thinking it was so absurd, so wild and outlandish, I worried I was going to start laughing. But it hurt; I can't pretend it didn't. I couldn't wait to go home, call my parents, and vent, a postcourt ritual that had *saved* me.

Moments later, following the opposing side's final argument, the judge made another ruling. It was a gag order. It is normal during a court battle for the opposing side to keep throwing out claims and accusations to see what might "stick," like throwing spaghetti noodles against the wall. Maybe the judge was tired, maybe he just wanted the chaos gone, but we were given no opportunity to respond. He just shut it all down with a gag order for everyone. I was floored. During the remaining court proceedings (which, spoiler alert, went on for another year and a half), I wasn't allowed to speak about what we were going through. I lost my voice. Legally. If I did speak about the case, our lawyer told us the repercussions would be serious. I kept quiet, as instructed.

The kids, who had been a part of every story and every adventure, and who I shared every part of my life with, disappeared from my social media accounts. People began to ask questions; they wondered where our kids went and wrote to make sure everything was okay.

"What happened to her children?" one commenter posted.

"Maybe she was just using them to get Instagram famous and now they're gone," another speculated.

I couldn't reassure anyone and nobody could reassure me. Because I couldn't speak up, I couldn't rally the support that I desperately needed. As the war raged on and more mud was slung, I began to feel alone. Before long, loneliness turned into depression, and depression to the belief that I was insignificant, invisible, and ultimately, powerless.

There was one small comfort in the harshness of it all, one brief moment of respite. Before each session, I went to the bathroom, stared in the gray, dingy mirror and made a promise to myself: when all this was over, whatever "over" looked like, I would tell my story.

Two silent years later, the fight inside the courtroom was over and I *was* finally able to use my voice again. The battle for our kids had ended, so there was nothing to protect anymore. I wanted to shine a light on the injustices of the court system, I wanted to share my experience with grief, let my community know that we had lost the children; I wanted to advocate for families just like mine that had been torn apart. But when I tried to speak, I quite literally could not! I'd open my mouth and begin to tell our story during interviews or at speaking events, but within seconds, I'd go mute. A lymph node on the right side of my throat would swell up to the size of a golf ball and I'd need to excuse myself.

The problem became increasingly worse. It began to crop up as I wrote blog posts, during everyday conversations, talks with my family, even sometimes with Mike. This visible lump in my throat acted as a barricade, the words I waited so long to say, the truth, was trapped behind.

I went to every type of specialist you can imagine, I had x-rays and MRIs. Nobody could find the root of the problem. After ruling out dangerous physical ailments, I began to focus on the emotional ones.

I went to my EMDR therapist and told her I felt like I had rocks in my throat. She nodded and smiled gently, "Maybe it's because you feel like your voice doesn't matter anymore? Or maybe, you're actually afraid of its power?"

That was it. I was told that if I spoke, I would be putting my children and my future in jeopardy. I might have felt powerless but the reason I was silenced, the reason I lost my voice, was because it was powerful. It was a new, fresh view of the situation that started to remind me of the importance of my voice.

I had forgotten about the power behind my voice. I used it to tell my children, "I love you." I used it to lift up other women. My voice built successful companies, created a strong relationship with the man I love, and advocated for the incredible kids that worked for the Shine Project. My voice was powerful and it was good. I didn't need to fear that power the way I had been told to; I needed to reclaim it. I felt like the little girl in Sunday school again; I was scared and suppressed, and reclaiming my voice would mean that I would need to reclaim the places in my life that I hadn't wanted to think about anymore.

For all of us, there will be times when our voices feel weak and tired, when we forget just how powerful, meaningful, and beautiful they can be. If you've forgotten, it's time to remember. If you've lost your voice, it's time to learn to sing again. It's time for all of us to get LOUD. Living with clarity means living with confidence. It means knowing your power, owning your power, and using it. There is somebody today who needs to hear what you have to say. There is somebody who needs you to be loud, to speak up, to freaking roar! And I want you to know that you have permission to be loud, and that people will hear you. Your seat at the table needs you in it, contributing and weighing in.

When nothing else seemed to work with restoring my

voice, I began experimenting with visualization, imagining my voice as something familiar and friendly that I could reach out and touch. When I visualize my voice, I like to picture it as something I can give to someone I love. It helps me remember that my voice has value, not just for me, but for others. More often than not, the thing that embodies my voice the best is a good old-fashioned pack of Skittles, my kiddos' very favorite snack. I remember their little squeals and the sound they made when they shook the bag, as though they were trying to guess how many candies were waiting for them inside. I remember how much joy such a simple little thing brought to them. If you're wondering if I just close my eyes and picture myself as some kind of happy, candy-breathing dragon, that isn't exactly how it works. I simply think of each word I say as something meaningful, beautiful, and *for* someone.

When I first began experimenting with this exercise, I would lose focus easily. The adorable rainbow candies would become heavy, gray rocks and that lymph node on my neck would start to throb against my jugular. When this happened, I would place a hand on my throat, recenter, say out loud, "You're safe," and continue. I did the exercise once every day and, always, in my dressing room before I would go onstage to speak. With practice and patience, using my voice became as familiar, fun, and joyful as surprising my kids with something sweet.

Not everybody likes Skittles (but really, who are you people?) and not everybody is going to like what I have to say. That's okay, as long the rainbow reaches those who can benefit from it. (Y'all, if I don't get a Skittles sponsorship after this . . .)

Within a few months of doing this, I became more confident and comfortable speaking than ever, and it showed. I began to receive more invitations to serve on panels and speak at conferences. The most magical thing of all, though, was that the more comfortable I was speaking my truth, the louder I proclaimed it, the more comfortable other women seemed to feel sharing their own. Audience members would come find me after events and share the hard stuff, openly, honestly, and without a hint of hesitation. I heard about grief and depression and loss. I heard about triumph and love and faith. What I saw and what I heard was women knowing, owning, and using their power. If you happen to be one of those incredible women who shared with me: thank you, I'm in awe.

Maybe you've lost your voice because you're feeling intimidated by a big conference presentation you have to give. Maybe your political views are a little different from those around you. Maybe you don't want to tell your boyfriend that you think his cologne smells less woodsy and more like a bunch of dirty camping gear. Maybe your gag order has just been lifted and you're afraid to open up. Whatever the reason may be, just because you've lost your voice doesn't mean you can't find it again. Here are three steps I take when I want to turn up the volume and dial down the fear:

1 **First breath, then voice.** When I connect to my breath, it always grounds me in the present moment. When I am grounded in the present moment, then I am able to clearly think about what I need to say right then, instead of being worried about how others will receive it, or wondering if it's okay to say, or questioning my ability to speak truth. Without fail, when I first focus on my breath, then I am able to more powerfully let out my voice. I breathe in deep for four counts, then I heavily exhale to the count of eight. I do this for two minutes, and it brings all my senses right into my current moment and gets my voice ready to be heard! The next time you have something intimidating to do or say, take a minute to find your breath. Try this exercise, breathing in for four counts and exhaling for eight. Then use your voice!

2 **Picture your power.** I often visualize myself on-stage. Sometimes there is nobody in the audience, and other times I'm in an arena full of people, and each time, I allow my power and my voice to hold the same amount of value. I picture myself shooting rainbows (literally!), from my mouth to the people in the audience who need some light and love, and I watch it transform the space that I'm speaking to. When I can picture my power, it allows me to feel that my voice is important, no matter whom I am speaking to. Visualize yourself speaking at a place of significance to you, and walk yourself through every detail of what it feels and looks like, so that you can make it a reality.

3   **Speak your truth!** Say it out loud, even if it's to yourself. Let the power of your voice surprise you, and give yourself permission to get loud. Proclaiming your voice is like exercising a muscle at the gym. The more you go, the stronger it gets, and the easier it becomes to let your truth out.

You are LOUD, you are a warrior of truth and light, and that rainbow gets to shine out of you forever and ever. I don't know the details of your life, I don't know the things that have made you believe that your voice isn't important or that you're not heard, but I want you to know this: your voice is powerful.

15

I AM NOT
Alone

If you have felt pain, loneliness, fear, uncertainty, or sadness in the past three years, will you please stand up?"

Pain sucked the air from the room. You could almost hear it. All five hundred of the women I was speaking to at the conference stood up. Dozens of women of all ages sprang to their feet and wept with relief and recognition, but others were slow and tentative to join. Some started crying, as though the admission was a secret they'd been keeping for years.

I asked them another question: "If you have felt alone today, during our time together, would you please raise your hand?"

Every single hand went up; some went up fast. I watched

them, eyes darting around and taking shallow breaths before daring to answer the question, before agreeing to introduce a shadowy part of themselves to a room full of strangers. Choosing to answer the hard questions is an act of courage.

Staring up at me were five hundred incredible, vulnerable, beautiful human beings standing side by side, just inches from one another. I wondered about them. Though the details may be different, they were united in so many of the same struggles and shared so many of the same fears. Still, though, as their arms touched and they shed tears in tandem, they all felt alone. I raised my own hand and felt my own eyes begin to fill with sadness.

Pain can isolate us, or, with a little bravery and a lot of humility, it can bring us together. In my experience, pain is a great teacher but not always a nice one. Often, it can make us feel totally alone. For me, loneliness is one of the most crippling feelings in the world, and it will take me from moving forward to flat on my face in seconds. There are a few things about aloneness I'd like to address:

1 Aloneness can happen when you're not alone. I can feel alone in a crowded room, I can feel alone in my husband's arms, I can feel alone writing about my aloneness. It's a lack of connectedness to the heartbeats that surround us. They can be there, but that doesn't mean that *we* are, that we feel seen by others, or even that we're able to see them.

2 **Aloneness can happen to anyone.** Your greatest hero has felt alone, the most popular girl in school, the celebrity you idolize. We all know what it is to feel vulnerable, and isolated. The feeling of aloneness is a reaction, not a reality. It's often a by-product of sadness, pain, or fear. It tricks us into thinking we're the only ones, and that we must wade through the tough days relying solely on our own strength.

3 **You are not alone. Not ever.** There is someone standing inches away who sees you, who shares struggles with you. She might not have her hand up, but she's right there.

Living with clarity and reclaiming your power isn't about banishing these alienating feelings, it's about accepting them, understanding them, and seeking comfort. While it's easy to feel isolated in this world when we're hurting, instead of making pain into the barrier that separates us from others, I believe we can make it the gateway.

When I feel alone and need reassurance. I repeat three steps: reach in, reach out, reach up. I'm going to show you how to remember your connection with yourself, your sister, and your god. I'm going to show that even when you feel alone, you're not. The story I'm about to share with you is still unfolding. It has reminded me how hard it can be to feel stuck and just how paralyzing feelings of true loneliness can be.

Step 1: Reach In

Three years after losing our kids, almost to the day, I found out I was pregnant. My period was late and I had what I thought was a sudden bout of food poisoning. I took a drugstore pregnancy test, then I took three more.

We were thrilled, bursting with joy, we couldn't keep the news to ourselves for even ten minutes. We ran to my family's house and told everyone. It felt so divine, the timing couldn't have been more perfect, and we were so excited to meet the little person in my belly. Growing our family after loss was a big, weighty decision that had taken us years to make, but surrounded by squealing family members and a glowing husband (that's right, for the first bit *he* was the one that glowed), I knew it was right.

I scheduled an appointment with my OB right away. My insurance required a doctor's note to confirm my pregnancy before I could enroll in maternity care, and I was ready, beyond ready, for that first scan.

The nurse practitioner listened to my symptoms on the phone, nodding and "uh-huhing." I was sick, exhausted, hormonal, and achy. Basically, a cartoonish rendering of all the pregnancy symptoms that a person can have. She wondered if I might be further along than we thought and suggested we do a quick ultrasound to see.

"If nothing else, it will be fun!" she sang, assuredly. She thought we'd all love seeing the progress of the pregnancy.

It turned out, though, it wasn't fun.

They performed an internal scan on Thursday morning with a very, very cold wand. We stared at the screen in awe looking for the little blips of life in the shadow. We saw a little circle, our little circle. I couldn't believe it. I was thrilled, but nobody else seemed to be.

The doctor came in afterward and told us my gestational sac was really small. There was no yolk sac in it yet, which wasn't typical. Something was wrong.

He ordered blood tests and left the room with a bleak-sounding, "Keep your fingers crossed." We were stunned.

Our wonderful nurse tried to reassure us. She rubbed my back and got Mike, who was white-faced and confused, one of the lollipops normally reserved for nauseous women in their first trimester.

We got home that night, and the feelings of peace, togetherness, and divinity that had me walking on clouds for the past couple of weeks evaporated. In their place was a familiar sadness: grief. The trauma of losing my kids returned to me; I felt as freshly wounded as I did that day three years ago. If the pregnancy wasn't viable, our family would be slipping away again. More than anything else, I felt alone. Even with a baby in my belly. Even with a husband by my side. Even with a family right down the street. Even with comfort and support within inches.

When these feelings come to me, the first thing I do is connect with myself. This is the "reaching in" step. I remind myself what's reaction and what's reality, and I listen. That day, I stood in front of my mirror and got quiet, making space for my intuition to speak to me. Instead of focusing on all the things I wasn't or might not be, I let my intuition bind me to the truth. I placed a hand on my belly and said, "I am a mother," out loud.

I knew that for myself and for my baby, I needed to wade past the muck and the uncertainties and go all in on the things I did know. I *knew* I was a mother, no matter what. I *knew* I was pregnant, and while I didn't know what the outcome would be, I *knew* I was still experiencing a gift. I was carrying life.

"I am not alone."

I looked down at my stomach just barely poking out over my jeans and thought about the little circle I'd met just hours before.

"*We* are not alone."

Reaching in allows me to focus on what's happening within, instead of around me. When I can connect to myself, things start feeling less confusing, less overwhelming, and a lot less out of control. Reaching in is giving ourselves the permission to feel safe and secure, even if there's a storm around us.

Step 2: Reach Out

We had our follow-up appointment exactly one week later. For seven days my nerves were buzzing, hoping our little one was growing, praying for a heartbeat, trying to grab ahold of peace. We had no idea what we were walking into as I sat on that same ultrasound table again and waited for the doctor to come in. Mike held my hand, and I flashed him a smile that ended with a giggle. We were about to see our baby, and no amount of fear could settle the excitement.

The doctor came in, the screen lit up, and we began. In a few moments, he turned to us baffled. "I have never seen this before. In all thirty-five years of practice, I don't know what this is."

On the screen inside the sac where the baby was supposed to be was a giant mass. "I'm sorry, but there's no heartbeat, and we need to determine what this mass is."

The doctor and the nurse left the room hurriedly. I sat

up, trying to inhale and exhale, inhale and exhale, but the deep sobs that rose in my throat kept me gasping. Not only had we lost our baby, but there was now a serious medical concern about my body.

The doctor came in and told us he sent the images to other specialists to rule out a life-threatening condition. He softened a little and told us he would let us know as soon as he knew more.

Since it was late in the day and I was not in immediate danger, they scheduled me for deeper imaging the next morning and sent me home to rest, taking my blood counts before I left in case I needed emergency surgery. I walked out of the exam room into a literal sea of pregnant bellies, hands over my face and snot dripping down my nose.

On our drive home I kept shaking my head, asking Mike why we kept getting knocked down every time we felt like we'd found our footing. We felt defeated. As we rolled along the interstate, I asked, "Where do we go from here?"

I just didn't know what the next right thing looked like. But he did.

Silently, he took the next exit and before I knew it, we were in my parents' driveway. When you don't know where to go, sometimes the answer is, simply, home.

We reached out, and our family cried with us. They prayed with us. They told us that they'd be right there as we moved through this and promised to help me heal physically and emotionally from whatever it was I was facing. I didn't have to carry the pain alone. None of us do.

It isn't easy to reach out. We get scared of other people's judgments, we don't want to burden the ones we love, we think our problems are unimportant, we think they think *we* are unimportant. We don't always know who to trust, who will understand, who will offer us the comfort and connection we so desperately desire. Sometimes, the only way to learn where to lean is to let yourself fall. You may be surprised how quickly someone will lift you. You won't know, though, unless you're willing to reach that hand up and ask for help.

Not everyone has an awesome family down the road. If this is you, you're still not alone. Reach out to a therapist (or twelve, like me), join a support group, find an online community that makes you feel seen and heard. Expanding your circle takes courage, but on the other side is where compassion lives.

Step 3: Reach Up

Before I fell asleep that night, I was trying to mentally prepare myself for what would happen in the morning. I mourned the loss of the baby, and also, I feared for my own life. I stared at the ceiling, planning the nursery one moment and a funeral the next. Mike walked in. "Ashley. We're not talking anymore about losing the baby. I believe a miracle will happen. I believe that in the morning, we will see the heartbeat."

I thought Mike had gone totally nuts. I was concerned for him, for what would he do in the morning when reality set in. How would he deal with the loss? I wondered if we had seen the same ultrasound or if he had completely checked out. Mike believed in his miracle; I barely believed I'd have the strength to make it through another appointment.

I know that, sometimes, reaching up is the hardest act of them all, but it may also be the most powerful. I know what it's like to feel abandoned by your Higher Power, to wonder why God has allowed certain things to happen to you, to question if there even is a God at all. I want to be sure that as I talk about reaching up, you know it's completely okay if our perceptions about who and what God is are different. What is most important to me is that you can trust in reaching up to a Higher Power, a Creator, a bigger source of light and love that can help sustain you, so that you know you are never, ever alone.

When we lost our children, my ideas of who God was were completely shattered. God no longer fit the description of the Creator who held my faith growing up. It became difficult for me to want to pray, and connect, and trust in God anymore. I felt tricked. My reality had been shifted and I began to wonder what was true and what wasn't. My relationship with the God I believed in felt so strained that it felt safer for me to just put it to the side for a while. I believed that if God was all loving, it would be okay if I was mad and took a break for a while.

I took a long break, but as I healed, I found faith again. I found faith again because I allowed it to become different than it was before. It didn't have to fit into a box anymore that had perfect answers. It didn't have to find the rainbow at the end of the storm that I used to desperately search for. Faith stopped being a miracle found at the end of a story and started being a power I'd hold on to in the middle of it. Faith became an acceptance. An acceptance that even when my world fell apart and there was no brilliant connection between the pain and a miracle, I was still deeply loved. That not "everything happens for a reason," but that I could get through it, no matter what. Suddenly, though, with a little life on the line inside me and possibly my own life in jeopardy, I felt doubt creep in.

It was a long drive to the radiologist the next morning. They opened the office early to fit us in and had a specialist in England waiting to review my scans the moment they were done.

My knees were shaking so badly in the stirrups that Mike had to hold them. I didn't want to see again what we had seen the day before, so I closed my eyes, waiting for it all to be over. As I shut my eyes, I prayed silently and simply, *Help*.

I heard a sound I never had before. It was like the thumping of a bass drum but stronger, steadier. Somehow, surer of itself. It was a heartbeat. I didn't know why the radiologist would be listening to *my* heartbeat, but I didn't ask any questions. My knees were knocking into each other at this point and my teeth were chattering. I wanted nothing more than to get dressed and leave.

A minute later, I heard the heartbeat again, fast and frantic. I opened my eyes and saw it on the screen.

"What is that?" I asked. "What's that heartbeat?"

The radiologist looked at me and said, "Why, that's your baby!"

"What do you mean, that's our baby? We don't have a baby. There was no heartbeat yesterday."

She responded with the most beautiful smile. "Well, the doctor must have missed it."

I had every type of scan humanly possible that day and when we left, the baby's heartbeat still ringing gloriously in my ears, the radiologist said, "You know, I don't know what's going on. But I think everything is going to be okay."

It was a miracle. We had our baby.

The specialist in England finally got back to us with

an answer. The mass inside of me was called a chorionic bump pregnancy, and we learned it happens in less than 1 percent of pregnancies and put me in a high-risk category, but many of these pregnancies turn out to be healthy. We did not know what was going to happen tomorrow, but we did know that some days, miracles can happen.

Reaching up can be terrifying but I also know, no matter what has happened in our lives, that we haven't been forgotten. No matter the outcome of my pregnancy, I know I am not alone. Reaching up starts with a small belief, choosing to put hope in front of our doubt. It's knowing that no matter what happens, even if the miracle doesn't come, we aren't alone.

At the end of my speaking event, I looked out at my audience again. I'd talked for an hour about our ability to shine, even in life's darkest moments, and I hoped that with that light, the beautiful, illuminated women before me could now see that they weren't alone. Some of the women were still crying. Others looked like they were re-kindled, ready to charge out of the conference room and into a whole new life. Before I closed my presentation, I asked them the same question I had at the beginning

"If you have felt pain, loneliness, fear, uncertainty, or sadness in the past three years, will you please stand up."

Just like they had at the beginning, every woman in the room stood up. This time, I told them to hold the hand of the person next to them. They were fully connected to themselves and to one another. I looked out at them, strangers holding strangers, strangers becoming sisters. The energy of the room felt completely different than the first time. I asked again, "If you still feel alone, would you please raise your hand?"

Not a single hand went up. Each held on tight to another.

16

I AM
Safe

It was March 2020, and the world felt like it was exploding. Your world, I can imagine, felt like it was exploding, too. COVID-19 was in its beginning stages of sweeping the entire world, and nobody knew what the future held. Businesses, schools, and entire communities were shutting down. The fear of the unknown, the quick collapse of so many dreams that had been built for decades, the lack of trust in our surroundings, and the confusion on what would happen next was incredibly overwhelming at best.

The first week that COVID hit the United States, we moved into a new home to mark a new chapter in our lives. Sixteen weeks pregnant, growing our roots back in Phoenix to be near our families and continue growing our own, it felt like a renewal during a time of so much upheaval. We felt safe in our home, and safe in the promise that our little family would soon be growing, despite what was going on around us.

Four days after we got the keys to our new house, I had spent the day planning the baby's nursery that would sit next to our bedroom and decided to rest by lying on the couch early in the evening. My legs had started cramping, so I called Mike in from his office and asked if he could rub them. I had been on my feet a lot that day since my morning sickness was finally starting to subside, and I thought my muscles were tired. By bedtime, the pain had moved into my pelvis, up through my back, and I had the chills. Since understanding around COVID was still so new, I didn't want to have to go to the emergency room. Mike went to the store to get me a fever reducer and some Gatorade. Two hours later, around midnight, I was screaming in pain. I knew I needed to get medical help, but I could not walk. Mike called an ambulance, and I was in the emergency room within the hour.

The first thing they did was take blood work, and then check on the baby. They wouldn't allow Mike into the ultrasound room with me because they were limiting people in the hospital due to the pandemic, so I lay alone on a cold, metal table, praying and pleading that I would hear my baby's heartbeat. Even though the tech wasn't allowed to confirm to me what was happening, I saw the heartbeat racing across the screen. I deeply exhaled, eternally grateful with every bone in my body that my baby was safe. I was wheeled back out to meet Mike in my room, as I screamed in pain. The doctor quickly came and met us. The good news was that the baby was perfect. The bad news was that I was septic from a strep B infection that had led to two kidney infections and was in my blood. I was confused. I hadn't had any prior infections, I was incredibly healthy, and I was fine just hours before.

That's when they told me to say good-bye to Mike. "What do you mean, say good-bye? He'll be coming with me." It was then we learned that just that day, in order to prevent the spread of COVID-19, the hospital was not allowing any guests past the emergency room if they were not the patient. I would have to go through the coming days entirely alone. Being wheeled away from my husband during the greatest physical pain I have ever endured was one of the most terrifying moments of my life.

At that time, there was one part of the hospital, the observation area, that hadn't been exposed to COVID patients. Because I was pregnant, they wanted to keep me as safe as possible, and also not have doctors who had been exposed working with me, so they put me in this part of the hospital. This was in the very early days of the spread of the disease, so nobody knew what to expect, and it was all very, very new. I was immediately put on IV antibiotics and told that I would have to have a PICC line put in, to administer the antibiotics for several weeks. Since I was pregnant, my options for pain medicine were slim, and I'm allergic to morphine, which means that for the next two days I would lie in bed, screaming, in the most horrific pain I have ever felt in my life. Although the baby was okay, due to the infection in my kidneys, my urine was bright red. They put a diaper on me because I could not get out of my bed, and the only thing separating me and the patients around me was a thin curtain. Which meant that every scream was heard by every patient on the floor.

I was willing to go through anything I needed to ensure the safety of my unborn child. Forty-eight hours into my battle with sepsis, the rapid response team was called in and I was quickly surrounded with a dozen doctors checking my heart, my lungs, my vitals, putting oxygen through my nose and sticking more needles in my arms. My entire body had gone numb. I could hardly breathe. I kept asking if I was going to die, or if I was having a stroke. I had never been afraid of death, until that moment when I thought that it was coming for me. The sweet doctor who was giving me my EKG test looked at me while I was screaming from pain, and said, "Nobody else can do as good of a job as you to get through what you need to get through. You're doing so good. Keep being you and breathe. This won't last forever."

My vitals started improving later that night. But I was deeply worried about my baby. My pain was still out of this world, and I did not know how both of us could survive what was happening. I asked for the maternity unit to come assess me again. They did. They told me I felt okay and my cervix was still closed, and I told them I wanted another ultrasound to be sure. They promised to send a Doppler up the next day with a nurse.

Twenty-four hours later, a Doppler and a young nurse finally arrived at my room. I was told it was an easy and quick process to give me peace of mind. But after two minutes of the Doppler being placed all over my stomach, the nurse said, "It's normal to not hear a heartbeat all the time on this machine. I'll order an ultrasound so you can see the baby that way."

This is the part of the story I do not want to tell. But in sharing, it has connected me with millions of women around the world who carry the pain of child loss. I sat in the ultrasound, alone, and scared. I knew what to look for on the screen, even though they couldn't confirm anything until a doctor was sent to tell me the results. I stared at the screen until the time came when my tech pulled up the heartbeat. He only had it pulled up for a quick second, but that's all we both needed to see its noiseless, flat pulse string across the screen. I went blurry. I sobbed uncontrollably as I was wheeled back to my "room" with the curtains. I waited for the OB to come and confirm the news.

"There is no heartbeat. This is something we take seriously before giving a definitive answer, so we will have you go for another scan in the morning. We need to get your body stable from the sepsis, and then we will consider our options on how to deliver the baby if that is what needs to happen. You have time." I begged the doctor and nurse to allow my husband to come and be with me that night. Nobody would let him in. My mom and sister drove to the parking lot of the hospital and sat there for hours while FaceTiming with me so that I would know I wasn't alone. I was so scared, I felt so unsafe in that hospital and inside of my own body, but there was no escaping.

The next morning, on Friday, March 27, my sweet baby boy made his quick and short entry into the world. I had been up all night having contractions and cramping. I woke up soaked in more blood and kept telling the nurses that I needed help. I kept telling them that I felt like I was in labor. Because I was still in the observation area, none of the nurses were trained in delivery.

The man who was giving me my PICC line procedure had shown up just minutes before I delivered my baby. I told him to not come through the curtain yet because I needed to use my bathroom. My toilet had been right on the side of my bed, since I couldn't walk any farther. As I sat over the toilet, I felt immense pressure, and saw that my baby was coming into the world. I was screaming for nurses. I was calling for help. By the time they came he was fully delivered, and I was too scared to look at him. I'm ashamed of how scared I was.

They put me and my baby back on my bed, and I waited to finally have the labor and delivery nurses and OB come. Mike was on the speakerphone with me when they arrived, and the first thing he asked was, "Is it a boy or a girl?" The OB replied, "It's a baby boy." Under my arm was placed a teddy bear so that my hands wouldn't be empty. As the baby and I were rushed through the hospital halls to the new unit where the moms around me were giving birth, I was told that my husband could finally come be with me. I have never been happier to see that man in my entire life.

We chose the name Jayce because it means healer. And I fully believe this baby came and healed parts of me that hadn't seen the light in decades. Michael, his middle name, was after his brave daddy. My family made posters and sat outside the hospital window since they could not be with me in person. And my labor and delivery nurses, those sweet angels, got me through the next three days of absolute hell.

There I was. Having lost our rainbow. Having lost our promise that the future does get better. Having been buried into the ground again, so deeply, that I couldn't even fathom getting back up as I was close to dying myself, I wanted nothing to do with this life anymore. I wanted none of it. After a week of being in the hospital, I was released to go home with a home nurse. Antibiotics were administered to me daily through my PICC line. I had to plan my baby's burial. I'd pass by the mirror and be disgusted with an empty, pregnant-looking belly that failed her baby. Every physical pain I felt sent me into a terror that my sepsis was taking over again. Nothing felt happy. Nothing felt normal. Nothing felt safe.

While the world was falling apart around us, my personal world was shattering as well. I had done so much healing, so much brutal internal work to get to a place where I was ready to grow our family again, and it all just exploded right in our face. Everything felt scary again. I had put so much trust back into the universe, into God, into a future filled with joy, that I hadn't even considered this outcome once we got pregnant. What kind of sick plan presents this as the outcome? My trust in everything around me felt so broken, so unsafe to exist, that my journey felt like not only was I now starting over in my healing process, but all the clarity I had thought I finally uncovered in my life was now more confusing than ever before.

I truly believe the words *I AM safe* can play a critical,

healing role in our lives. I have learned that because pain has come once doesn't mean it won't come again. This is something that can leave us frozen in fear or can prepare us to keep knowing how to handle and learn from pain when it comes. Living in fight-or-flight mode is exhausting, painful, and detrimental to our physical, spiritual, and emotional health. So how do we feel safe with ourselves and the world when everything feels so scary? Here are three small things I do:

1 **Look for the lullabies.** While in the hospital, a nursery song would play every few hours. I noticed it my first night there, and hearing it brought me so much peace. I asked the nurse what it was for and she told me it played every time a baby was born. I kept listening for the lullaby those first couple of days, and every time I'd hear it, I'd tell myself that in a few months, that song would be played for my baby. It gave me courage to withstand the pain that overtook my body.

Within the hour of delivering Jayce, the lullaby came on. I'd hear it multiple times a day through the remainder of my stay. Instead of bringing pain, it brought me so much hope. It reminded me that life still grows, that there is still joy, and love still exists, even in our darkest moments. It was a promise that life was still surrounding me.

Every day since we left the hospital, I look for the

lullabies throughout my day. Sometimes it's the sun coming up, or the butterfly that flutters past my window; other times it's my husband's laugh or the feeling of my own smile breaking through.

I know that life might seem unsafe and impossible right now for you. But I also know that some little lullabies are still surrounding you. They are creating a net of safety so that you can remember life still exists around you, and that love and joy can overpower the darkness. Listen for the lullaby today.

2 **Acknowledge when you make a good decision.** Learning how to trust myself again, to feel safe within my own body, and to trust my intuition after I felt like it led me so astray has been one of the hardest things I've ever had to do. How do you feel safe in your life when you don't feel safe with yourself? It's easy to second-guess ourselves, to look outward for answers instead of inside, and to get frustrated with who we are because it just seems like we can't get it right. To help show myself that a powerful pattern of good decisions that I have made actually has led to good outcomes, I physically write down when I've made a good decision. I let it live on a piece of paper, with all the other good decisions I've made, so that whenever I need a reminder that it is safe to trust my intuition, I look at all the times it has led me to just where I needed to be. This starts with acknowledging that our voice and actions are powerful and impactful and help give us more confidence in ourselves. And confidence brings a feeling of safety and security.

3 **Understand that you are not starting over again.** I used to believe that when we experienced pain again in our lives, it moved us right back to the starting line where we began. I would feel like I had made so much progress, only to lose all of my healing work when the next painful moment came. I viewed pain as linear, like a race forward. But pain is more like a staircase, spiraling upward. You might feel, sometimes, like you're starting all over again, but really, you are now a few flights of stairs up, you've been climbing all along, and so now you continue on with new tools, a new perspective, and a deeper power to overcome than you had before.

When I remember that my pain is a staircase, I feel safe in knowing that every experience I have can lead me further up my climb, and it doesn't take me back to the beginning. It took me a while to realize it, but what we're climbing toward is our truest self. And that's actually the safest place to be.

I've shared with you a couple of mantras that I've used to help guide me through my healing and uncovering clarity in my life, and I want to leave you with this one. Put your hands right on your neck, so you can feel the deep vibrations of your voice, and say the words out loud, *I am safe. I am safe. I am safe.*

You have permission to find safety in yourself, in your surroundings, and in your healing. You are safe to keep climbing.

17

I AM THE
Rainbow

As I struggled with the loss of my baby boy, I talked with my doctor about how the wave of grief felt more like a tsunami at all times of the day instead of being an ebb and flow that allowed me to catch my breath, and I was diagnosed with postpartum depression. My hormones were taking over, unneeded milk supply had come in, the infections in my body continued without answers, and my exhaustion kept me in bed for weeks at a time. I was telling a mentor that I just wanted my rainbow to come. It had been what felt like years of living through the storm. This was supposed to be our rainbow, our moment to feel safe to inhale the blessings of life again and reignite ourselves. I wanted my baby, my children, my joy, my health, my old body, whatever it was that was going to bring that rainbow; I wanted it, and I wanted it right now. Floods of messages were sent to me with love and support, many of which told me that they'd be praying for my rainbow baby to come.

In addition to my primary care doctors, I sought out other things that I hoped would fix me. I was taking over twenty vitamins and supplements a day, ate things to give me a momentary sugar high to feel good, watched shows in my bed that allowed me to escape my current reality, and felt like I was running in constant circles. I had stepped into the same pattern that I experienced after losing our older two kids: seeking outside of myself for anything that would fix my pain.

As I was asking what else I could do, who else I could go to for help, my mentor told me something that shifted my entire perspective on what it means to have the rainbow come. She said, "Ashley, what if the rainbow is YOU. What if you need nothing else, except for everything that you have inside? The pains you feel, what if they are fireflies, lifting you higher than you've ever been, bringing you more light as you see life from a different viewing point? The rainbow doesn't have to wait to appear until a new baby comes, or this other thing happens; Ashley, this is leading you to your rainbow! It's you!"

The rainbow was me. It wanted me to uncover it. The pot of gold I was chasing to find actually was inside of me all along. The hardest first step was allowing myself to get really still. Instead of seeking answers and numbing things to pacify my pain, I stopped trying to fill the void. I allowed the void to exist. I noticed the feelings and instead of trying to rush through them, I processed them. I learned to ask my own body questions like, *What do you need right now? How can I best serve those needs?* I would write my answers down. Some of them shocked me, because they were so profound, yet so simple, and as I would do the things my intuition told me I needed, I experienced more healing. As I noticed that stillness brought me answers, I started learning how to trust myself again. The body that I thought had failed me was actually leading me to exactly what and who I needed: myself.

I discovered new types of exercises that better supported my body healing. I learned that I was allergic to certain foods that were causing serious internal problems and completely changed the way I ate and my relationship with food to better serve my healing. I stopped trying to distract myself and really leaned in to listening to myself. It turns out, my intuition is a really great guide that led me to finding answers to pain that even my doctors hadn't been able to identify. Distraction was a reaction to my pain. But stillness was an invitation to learn what it was trying to teach me. And it was teaching me that I was the rainbow all along.

The rainbow is you. The gift you are waiting to receive,

the promise of a better tomorrow, the peace and comfort of safety, the freedom you're longing to feel, the light at the end of the tunnel you hope to find: it's all inside of you. The moment you find yourself currently in is the moment you've been waiting for your entire life. It's the moment that is lifting you higher, it's pushing you to uncover what you've always been searching for, and the pot of gold at the end of the magnificent rays of color is you.

18

I AM
Free

I used to think that time healed our wounds for us. I mean, that's what we're told will happen, right? If we can just be patient and wait for more distance to elapse between us and the moments that hurt us, eventually we'll be okay again. Everything will return to what it once was. Maybe we'll even laugh about it. Maybe it's a blessing in disguise.

Honestly, if I ever hear "Time heals all wounds" again, I am going to punch something in the face.

Time doesn't heal us, healing heals us. Sometimes the longer we sit by and wait for the pain to subside, the more power it has over us. The longer we wait, the more we pine for what was instead of imagining and experiencing what could be. In some cases, I'm sure distance may help ease an aching heart, but maybe healing is more about relief. Maybe healing isn't about what we don't feel and, instead, is about what we do. Maybe in healing there's room for grief and joy, sorrow and ecstasy, missing the ones you love and holding the memories close.

Even after years of writing, reflection, and healing, I have had days when I wanted my old life back, when I wanted to return to a time before the kids, before the courts, before grief, trauma, and loss. For a long time, I believed that's what healing was, a return—to a better time, a better place, a better feeling. Mostly, I believed that healing was the return to a better *me*.

I don't believe that anymore.

Healing isn't about going back to a time before pain; it's about finding the freedom, the courage to move forward with it. It's about realizing that we don't need to let go of everything holding us back to take the next step forward. (Remember, we talked about this earlier. You held those tender moments of yours with kindness, and I'm so proud of you I could burst.) Life is a messy, beautiful process and it's hardly just one thing—good, bad, joyful, heartbreaking—though I can't tell you the amount of times I've caught myself saying "Great!" when somebody asks how things are going. How do you pick a single word to describe this utterly magnificent, constantly evolving existence?! You can't, you don't, you've never, ever had to.

You can feel joy *and* grief. Pleasure *and* pain. Resilience *and* frustration. I learned this writing *Born to Shine*, and the freedom it's given me to feel everything without shame or regret has been such a gift. Healing doesn't mean not hurting, it means we tend to the wound.

I believed that writing and releasing *Born to Shine* would be the final step in my own healing journey. For months, I pushed and pulled and hemmed and hawed over what was important to include and what wasn't, over whether it was even ethical to release a book filled with lessons when I still had so, so much to learn. Speaking of ethics, I also wanted to be careful not to tell the details of my kids' lives, but they were so deeply intertwined with mine that it took a lot of sifting. One moment I wondered whether I should scrap the whole thing, and the next I wondered whether it would win an award. Even after I submitted the book, I had lingering doubts about it. There's nothing more vulnerable than sending in words that will be printed on pages for other people to read and criticize for the rest of your life. It felt like my heart was being handed over to strangers, and I was trusting that they weren't going to smash it into a million tiny pieces.

The one question that tortured me was a simple one. I would sit at my desk in the thick of edits and icky problem paragraphs and last-minute changes and ask myself: *Ashley, how do you feel about this?*

I couldn't decide. Was it a sad book or a happy book?

Was it a book about love or about loss? Was the reader going to walk away feeling uplifted or stitched to the ground?

Honest to God, I just didn't know. Deadlines came and went. I booked the tour, signed off on the cover design, and with a deep breath and the absolute *nicest* prodding my publisher could muster, I sent it in. Nearly fifty thousand words and about a million mixed emotions. I still couldn't decide how I felt about it.

One afternoon, an enormous camel-covered box arrived on the porch. I could smell the ink, fresh newspaper, and new car all in one as soon as I opened the door. A lump arrived promptly in the middle of my throat. I knew it was my book.

I slipped my scissors under the tape and carefully tore along the tiny bit of plastic separating me from my memoir. The flaps stretched themselves up toward the sky and there it was. The cover was a glossy midnight blue and felt smooth under my fingers. I had designed it and it looked even better in person than I could have imagined.

I pulled a copy out from the rest, and suddenly, fear took over. I could hold it. I could look it up and down. I could take a picture with it and post it on Instagram, but for some reason, I couldn't actually look inside. The permanence of the words I'd shared terrified me. Was it a testament to our love or the obituary of our family? I still didn't know how I felt.

A big humid breath of Tennessee summer floated by and I pulled the box, ungracefully, inside. As I did, the book I was sizing up flew to the floor and the dedication page was staring up at me.

Front door still wide open, box perching clumsily on the door threshold, I sat down beside it. I picked up the book that had so insistently opened itself for me and I read:

For Mike, S, and Z.
Thank you for teaching me how to shine in the darkest
night. I love you to the moon and back. Forever.

I felt absolutely everything—broken, whole, happy, sad, terribly lost, exactly where I was supposed to be.

I wept onto the tender words I'd written to the loves of my life and watched the paper dapple. I felt everything. For the first time, I knew that it was totally okay to feel that way. If I did have to pick one word as I sat and stared into the pages, it would have been *free*.

I had written the most important words in the book before the book even began, and every word that followed was put to paper with love. I was moving forward and I was taking the most beautiful parts of my past along with me. The people who had been with me through the darkest and hardest parts of my life were also the people who had given me the greatest source of light. And no matter where we all were, I didn't have to let them go. As I read that dedication page, I realized that nothing else mattered. I had written that book for them, and for myself. No other judgments or even praise mattered. And I promised myself that I would never read them, because I didn't want the weight of either of the sides to take away from the knowledge I had that I wrote every word in that book straight from my soul, my wonderful complex, happy, sad, beautiful, heartbroken soul.

When the book was released, I felt peace.

In this final chapter, I want to share the strategies I use to stay connected to that peace and move forward when the path gets mucky. It's so easy to feel as though you have to be on one side of healing or the other, but friends, I believe we're all in the midst of it. We can move forward *and* look back, we can hold great happiness in one hand *and* great sorrow in the other; it may complicate the journey but it also enriches it. You are free to move forward carrying whatever it is that you feel.

When I begin to feel myself stuck, questioning the journey, or overwhelmed with emotion, I get still and ask myself the one question I used to dread: *Ashley, how do you feel?* I keep these three words in mind when answering: *And. Now. So.*

And: You can feel joy and grief. Pleasure and pain. Excitement and trepidation. When I answer that question, I make a point of never settling for a single word. For some reason we live in a world that wants to define who we are so definitively that it's easy to believe we must be this, or we must be that. The good news that has liberated me is that we don't have to choose! The word *and* has become my lifeline, and my permission that I can have, and be, both.

Now: The word *now* has been so helpful in aiding me to remember that my emotions are as free to change and evolve as the rest of me. I might say to myself, *Now, I feel tired and nervous.* By the next morning, the next moment even, I might be feeling something entirely different. Our emotions aren't permanent. I know that it's easy to believe on bad days that our entire lives are bad, but it's just one hard moment, and as soon as *now* passes, we can begin to feel another way. Remembering that how I feel now won't be how I feel later empowers me to not go down a dark thought spiral that talks me into believing my life is hopeless or helpless. *Now* gives me my power back, because the present moment is the only place I have control over my emotions.

So: Addressing an effect or action that follows the emotions I've just identified helps me to remember that I am free to move forward with them. For example, if I answer with *I feel sad and lonely*, I'll complete the thought with *so I'm going to call my dad.* So creates a bridge of action; it is a powerful way forward when you feel stuck in a feeling or a problem. *I am devastated that I didn't get that job offer, so tonight I am going to relax in a bath, and tomorrow I will look for a new opportunity.* The word *so* creates SO many more options for our lives. Allow it to propel you forward, and that little word will get you more unstuck than you could believe!

Try it out. *And. Now. So.* Three words that can free you from so much baggage.

I know what it feels like to be chained to fear, held hostage to doubt, and buried by the uncertainty of the future. Pain can start making us feel like we're in bondage to something we have absolutely no control over, and waiting for a miraculous day where it all simply disappears is sometimes the only choice we feel like we have. But you can live free. Free from the heavy burden of all the things and moments that have ever made you feel too afraid to move forward in your life. With freedom from the pain past, and freedom from the fear of the future, you can move freely into the life that is waiting for you to grab it with both hands and boldly show up for. Doing that work for your life will be the most liberating, life-giving, and freeing choice you will ever make, and look at you, you've already made so much progress during our time together. There's a life that is waiting for all of us, where the extremes that we feel can teach us not only that we can live through the hard stuff, but that it was never supposed to destroy us. Our best lives are a mix of it all. Pain and joy, love and loss—we have to experience it all to rise above it all. And once we can rise above it all, then we are free. *You* are free.

Get Your Hands Up

"Put your hands up! You can keep crying, but you keep those hands up!"

Mike and I were in the master bedroom in a house in Memphis. We decided, on a whim, that it would be a good investment, something we could renovate and turn into the best Airbnb the birthplace of rock 'n' roll had ever seen. We weren't exactly Mr. and Mrs. Fix-it. In fact, we'd call a handyman just to hang a photo on the wall. We'd never taken on a full-scale reno before, and our parents and friends had tried to talk us out of it. They couldn't. Because Mike and I are excellent at talking ourselves into just about any kind of crazy idea.

Our contractor was two months late finishing. Every week we were given a strange new bill for a service we didn't even understand (what the heck is a subfloor anyway? Joanna Gaines never talks about subfloors!). By the end, the total cost was thousands of dollars higher than the original quote, and we were stunned. It was official, we were the proud owners of a grass-fed grade-A money pit.

Tennessee in the wintertime is dead and cold. After receiving the stack of bills in the mail, we drove three hours from Nashville to check out the progress. I was already crabby from the car ride and staring out at the uninspiring swaths of gray that rolled by out the window. We unlocked the door, and it was a disaster. The contractors hadn't bothered to cover our brand-new furniture, so everything was covered in dust, and chalk, and paint, and whatever else was flying around from chopping up a sixty-year-old home. There was no heat. I was going to have to sleep in my mittens, if we could sleep at the house at all. I started to lose it. That's probably the nicest way for me to put it.

On top of all the demolition drama, bigger issues were floating around the periphery. I had a book release to plan, Mike had coaching clients who needed him, and we were right in the thick of the season when our children had left us years ago. For us, winter always feels like it lasts a solid hundred years. For weeks, I hadn't been myself. I was distant and defeated. I felt lost again, and my body was responding poorly to a cocktail of the old traumas and the new pressures. My stomach felt like it was on fire, my head was spinning, my heart raced at night when it was supposed to be resting. I was just a heartbroken mom who wanted nothing more! than to hold her children. Instead, I was stuck inside a gutted Craftsman searching desperately for any feeling of home.

My husband held on to my shoulders and looked me dead in the eyes. I'd been bawling hysterically for about an hour in the half-finished bathroom and I could hardly see his face through the tears.

Mike led me into the master and sat me on the bed next to a stack of artwork that needed to be arranged on a shelf that needed to be anchored to the wall. I wanted to keep going, keep moving, but like I had felt many times in the past, my body and my mind felt disconnected. I was running in place. Grief is the ultimate treadmill; it convinces you that you're moving forward but when you stop for a second, you realize you're exactly where you were when you started. And you're exhausted.

Mike saw what was happening to me. He gently yet powerfully demanded, "Ashley, I need to know that you're here. I think you need to know it too."

He stood me up, holding me under the armpits.

"Put your hands up" he instructed.

I didn't want to, but I rooted my feet into the ground and tried. At first, he held my hands up for me. "I'm going to ask you to repeat something."

I nodded at him as he cleared his throat and roared, "I am strong! I am here!"

My arms felt heavy and my body felt weak and all I wanted was to ball up on the bed and retreat.

"It's your turn now."

Shaking, I stretched my arms toward the freshly painted ceiling. "I am strong. I am here." My voice shook.

"Again," he said.

"I am strong! I am here," I yowled, slightly louder.

He asked me to repeat it over and over. I'm not sure whether it was the sound of my own voice or the ache in my arms, but the more I said it, the more truth I felt in the words. Mike was right. I was showing up for myself, even though it was hard, even though I felt scared and alone. I was still showing up. There's dignity in *just showing up*. Sometimes we forget that.

As I held my arms in the air, I returned to Europe, to sprinting through Florence, to running and running until my spirit gave out, to the very moment I stopped running and chose to start participating. It reminded me that even in the hard seasons, the long gray days, there is still so much beauty.

I hope that in the pages of this book you have found some inspiration and tools to help you move past whatever has been keeping you stuck. That you feel equipped to reframe your negative thoughts and embrace what your pain has to teach you, and know that you are worthy of living a meaningful life. That you have the tools through the Clarity Mapping exercise to map out what's important in your life and act from that, so that you don't have to feel trapped by the circumstances of your life and can become the creator of it. By living from this intention, this purpose, I believe you'll start to see real change take place.

I'm not asking you to celebrate the people, things, and experiences that have hurt you. But they don't have to chain you down anymore. You have a new story to write, a new joy to uncover, and new freedom to live in a way that sets your soul on fire. Once you've acknowledged the impact your past had on you, let it empower you to make an impact on the world around you. Ask yourself next, *How can I use it to create change for someone else?* It might mean volunteering; it might mean reaching out to somebody you haven't heard from in a while. It might mean listening to a friend, I mean really, *really* listening. You can make a difference. And when you need a reminder of this, remember your affirmations and let them empower you: you are a fighter, you are loud, you aren't alone, you're safe, you're the rainbow, and you are free.

∾

"Get Your Hands Up" has become a practice Mike and I use often. It reminds us that we're still showing up for life, every single day. You don't need to summit the mountain to celebrate the climb. It's time for you to celebrate.

Friend, I want you to try it right now.

Stand up.

Lift your head and pull your shoulders back. Feel yourself rooted so firmly to the earth that the strongest wind couldn't move you.

Clench your hands into a fist.

Now, put your hands up over your head. And now, I want you to yell, "I am strong! I am here!"

Say it as many times as you need to, until you *feel* it in your bones. I want you to understand the magnitude of the importance of this moment, this day. Today, you showed up for yourself. Today, you chose to stay rooted.

You can cry, you can shake, but don't you dare put those arms down. Don't you dare forget where you are and the work you've done to get here. Whenever you feel weak or tired, whenever you feel like you don't have a place in the world, I want you to put your hands up wherever you are, and claim that space as your own. I want you to show up and announce your arrival.

Get those hands up. You are here and you are in the midst of your greatest victory.

Acknowledgments

There's a whole bunch of really amazing people who have made this book a reality. I thank you with my whole, entire, grateful soul.

Alexander Field—for taking a chance on me when it felt like my chances were up.

Katy Hamilton—for believing in these words and allowing me to use my voice in a way that's true to me.

HarperOne—for bringing to life the dream I had since I was eight years old.

Mike—for everything. And a dang good cover photo.

Jayce—for healing me in ways I never knew were possible.

Rebecca—for helping me find myself again, and guiding me to my rainbow.

R—for sitting with me as I discovered my Skittles.

Emily—for bringing my body and soul back to life.

Shannon—for helping me find the right words.

Alex and Summer—for being the constant light and joy that you are.

Acknowledgments

Z—for giving me life.

Brooke—for being my truest sisto.

Chandler—for your strong leadership and love for others.

Mom—for breaking the cycle.

Dad—for my love of writing, and dancing like a lunatic.

Ty—for the example that it's never too late to keep working for a dream.

Chrishana—for the loyalty and love you freely give.

The LeMieux family—for the unwavering support, and raising really great humans.

Randy—for teaching me how to show up for others.

Brittany—for being on this one-in-a-million journey (of all kinds) with me.

Alison—for being there in all my low and high moments the past several years.

My online community—You are the reason any of this exists. I go to bed and wake up thinking about you, and it is my privilege to be able to share my life and healing with you.

About the Author

Brenna Lee Photo, LLC

Ashley LeMieux is a grief and mental health expert and bestselling author of *Born to Shine*. Her online community is a place for women to find support, resources, motivation, and community to triumph over the challenges in their lives. She has empowered hundreds of thousands of women to find purpose in their pain and is the host of top-rated *The I Am Podcast*. Her passion for foster care reform has put her on the board of directors for the nonprofit National Angels. Ashley lives in Phoenix with her husband and baby girl.